"Father Wenig has caught the [...] *Joyful Expectation* provide [...] reflections and prayers for each day of the season and for each Sunday of the three-year cycle.

"With it you can venture forth through the longings and anticipation of Isaiah, John the Baptizer, and the Blessed Mother. It will take you right up to Christmas day in the finest liturgical style. A treat for priests, religious, and laity alike."

Msgr. Charles Dollen
The Priest

"Fr. Wenig brings to his reflections a scholar's insights and a pastor's practical spirituality. Informed by living in Israel and by dialogue with the Jewish people, the author is able to bring a vividness to the Hebrew Scriptures and a sense of the concrete setting of the New Testament that is both appealing and enriching."

Dr. Eugene J. Fisher
Associate Director, Secretariat for Ecumenical
and Interreligious Affairs

"Commenting on the Scriptures of the Mass during the Advent season, Fr. Wenig provides a joyful wake-up call to celebrate the beginning of the church's new year. *In Joyful Expectation* is a well-written gem; its vivid imagery and thoughtful questions for reflection will stimulate the Christian family to share and discuss God's word proclaimed in our own time."

John Burke, O.P.
Director, The National Institute for the Word of God

"In this delightful book, Father Wenig draws fruitfully on his experiences as rural pastor, a teacher of Scripture, and a former resident of Jerusalem. These simple, well-crafted reflections are filled with his love for Advent. True to the scriptural texts and directed to the lives of Christians today, they will be invaluable to those who seek to grow spiritually during the seasons of Advent and Christmas."

Rev. Gordon F. Davies
St. Augustine Seminary
Toronto, Ontario, Canada

IN JOYFUL EXPECTATION

Advent Prayers and Reflections

Laurin Wenig

Foreword by Rembert G. Weakland, OSB

XXIII

TWENTY-THIRD PUBLICATIONS
Mystic, Connecticut 06355

Twenty-Third Publications
185 Willow Street
P.O. Box 180
Mystic, CT 06355
(203) 536-2611
800-321-0411

ISBN 0-89622-596-8
Library of Congress Catalog Card Number 94-60310
Printed in the U.S.A.

FOREWORD

Often people apologize for keeping me waiting. I can exhibit a schizophrenic kind of reaction when I am kept waiting. If I am stuck with nothing to keep busy about, I can fret. If, on the other hand, I have a good book with me or am at home with a thousand chores I want to get done, I rejoice when I am being kept waiting. In fact, I see it as a blessing. (I usually am not bold enough in such cases, however, to say I was glad that the other was late; but I often feel that way. It is like an unexpected snow day.)

One day, as Abbot Primate of the Benedictine Confederation, I concluded a visit to a monastery that was located on an island and was ready to go on to the next community. The abbot of the monastery I was about to visit came to fetch me and drive me there. As we approached the entry ramp to put our car on the ferry that was to take us from the island to the mainland, I noticed at once that the "full" sign had gone up. We had missed the ferry and would have to wait hours for the next one.

We paced, we had a coffee, we fretted. All the abbot's plans for my grand entrance during community recreation had been frustrated. The hours dragged on and on as we tried to reconcile ourselves to the delay.

Right behind us was a carload of college kids, who, figuratively, were in the same boat we were in. They laughed, however, were glad to have the extra time, took out a frisbee and enjoyed the waiting.

You see, there are two different kinds of waiting. One is sterile. You sit and do nothing and time hangs heavy. The other is "busy" waiting. You are waiting but there are things to be done.

When I was in high school I recall having women relatives whose husbands or boyfriends were in the Pacific or European front during World War II. Each day, these women would write a long, very long letter to their loved one. Nothing ever happened in our hometown, but they seemed to find so much to say. Pictures of their loved ones were placed in strategic places in their homes, so that they and everyone who came in could see them, ask how they were doing, and get the latest news from the last letter received.

When word came that the boyfriend or husband was to return home soon, all the women went to the beauty parlor, to the dentist, to the stores. They spruced up the house, painted and varnished. For days they were busy getting everything in order.

Advent is a time of waiting, but not sterile and empty waiting. It is a time of creative expectancy. Letters are to be written, the house is to be put in order, so to speak. We are busy during Advent as we wait.

First of all, we know that we must get ourselves ready for the coming of Christ. Our letters written each day are our prayers. We pour out our musings as to one we love who is to come back. We know that Christ is with us, but we also know that the full presence of the Risen Lord is never totally a part of our consciousness and our actions. Advent brings that presence into our daily lives so that at Christmas we can say that God is more a reality to us than before we began our waiting.

We learn how to wait by meditating on how the people of old waited for the Savior. We become one with them. We learn to pray as they prayed.

We know that there is a Second Coming, but many do not like to think of that moment. It is important in our personal lives to do so; it is important for this world that we do so. Advent does not let us avoid the realization that the world is transitory and that Christ will come again.

For so many of us the apocalyptic literature that we read during Advent seems full of allusions and metaphors that are not meaningful to us. We tend, then, to put out of our minds the final coming of Christ. But Advent is a good time to take seriously the coming that we pray for each time we recite the Our Father.

Just as we prepare ourselves for the coming of Christ into our lives, so we must prepare this world for the final coming.

How do we do so? The response is simple: by acting justly toward others and by trying to create a society built on love and justice instead of on greed and selfishness. We try to create a world in which Christ would be at home. That is, we obey the commandments, especially those that point out how we should relate to others, how we must treat others.

Jesus comes at Christmas and at the end of time as the Prince of Peace. This means that we must imitate his healing presence so that he will find a world of peace and justice. We do so with acts that are just and full of peace. We do not just sit and wait, but creatively try to build a world based on love and unselfishness. Advent gives us the time to reflect on the need for such actions and how we can live justly in society.

Father Laurin Wenig's book will help us with this. *In Joyful Expectation: Advent Prayers and Reflections* provides just the right material for a good Advent. There are meditations for the Sundays of Advent for each year of the Lectionary cycle, and for every weekday of Advent. They are on all the virtues needed to prepare ourselves and this world creatively and wisely for the fullness of God's presence among us.

There is one last note, however. The reason why our

waiting is not usually fruitful is that we are too busy with non-essentials. Often that is a way of distracting us from the essentials. I can find a thousand things to do when I have to do something that requires discipline and that at first seems arduous.

Waiting creatively during Advent requires a time commitment and discipline. We have to get out of our cars, take out our frisbees, and not expect that it will just all happen on its own. Everyone in North American society is too busy today. Waiting creatively is a decision to set aside the time to reflect on how we should be using our time well. It takes a new kind of discipline to wait well.

My prayer will be that all the readers of *In Joyful Expectation* will persevere to the end. If so, then they will be much more conscious of God's presence in their lives this Christmas and this world of ours that God loves so dearly will be a better place in which to live and more ready to receive Christ again.

Most Rev. Rembert G. Weakland, O.S.B.
Archbishop of Milwaukee

PREFACE

Maranatha! "Come, Lord Jesus!" This simple Hebrew word summarizes the faith of the church. We are waiting for the Lord to come again.

Early Christians expected the return of the Lord to take place very soon, surely within their lifetime. How surprised they would be to find us, twenty centuries later, still waiting! The liturgical season we call Advent, The Coming, offers a rich feast of bible readings for our reflection and growth. Day after day the readings draw us into the mood of hopeful expectation that marked the messianic yearnings of ancient Israel.

At the same time, we know and believe that faith does not call us only to look backward. Advent also inspires us to look toward the Second Coming of Jesus and to prepare both our souls and our world for that glorious moment.

As mysteries will do, all this backward and forward viewing also inspires us to look more deeply into the present moment and to discover the presence of Jesus in the people, places, and events of our everyday lives.

This book of reflections originated as a series of personal meditations on the Advent readings. The Sunday reflections were first printed in the *Catholic Herald*, the weekly newspaper of the Archdiocese of Milwaukee. The daily meditations are reflections offered to the congregations of St. Matthew in Neosho and St. Mary in Woodland, Wisconsin, where the author serves as pastor. Because the author writes from his experience of living in Wisconsin, he makes occasional references to snow and cold. Those of you living in "snowless" climates can focus on the images of increasing darkness and desert solitude used throughout this book.

May the words of these meditations help you to find the presence of Jesus during this holy season. Maranatha!

How to Use This Book

This book contains a two-page reflection for each day of the Advent Season based on the readings used in the Liturgy of the Word at Mass on that day.

The bible verses for each day's readings are listed at the beginning of the meditation. Several questions for reflection, discussion, or action can be found at the end of each Sunday meditation. Each weekday reflection ends with a brief prayer.

Determine a time each day when you will read the reflection. Mornings seem to be best for most people. It can be as soon as you wake up, immediately before you leave the house, or while riding the bus or train to work. If time permits, read the bible passages that will be used at Mass that day. Husbands and wives or entire families may want to read the daily reflection together. During the day, call to mind the prayer or thought-provoking questions that conclude the reflection. You may want to read the meditation again later in the day to ponder the new insights that have touched your heart during the course of the day.

It is easy to use this book for each of the days of Advent. You should note, however, that the Advent Season takes on a slightly different time frame each year, depending upon the day of the week for Christmas. Thus, the Fourth Week of Advent is shorter in some years than others. There are a few other things to note:

Sundays: Because the church uses three sets of Sunday readings (A,B,C) in rotating fashion, this book has three different reflections for each Sunday of Advent.

In Advent 1995, 1998, 2001 use the reflections for Sunday —Year A.

In Advent 1996, 1999, 2002 use the reflections for Sunday —Year B.

In Advent 1994, 1997, 2000 use the reflections for Sunday—Year C.

Weekdays: There is one reflection for each day of the week. Use these for each weekday until December 17th.

Beginning on December 17th: Use the reflection for the corresponding dates from December 17th to 24th.

Additional Feast Days: These meditations are at the back of the book in calendar order. On these days, you may prefer to read the special meditation for the feast rather than the Advent Season reflection.

Sound confusing? It is really quite simple. And remember, the most important thing is very basic: Take time each day to welcome Christ into your life in this holy season of Advent. Maranatha. Come, Lord Jesus!

Contents

Advent is a time of waiting, but not sterile and empty waiting. It is a time of creative expectancy.

Most Rev. Rembert G. Weakland, O.S.B.

IN JOYFUL EXPECTATION

Advent Prayers and Reflections

THE FIRST WEEK OF ADVENT

The season of Advent has returned. It is the church's New Year's celebration. On this Sunday, year after year, we begin new things. We begin a new cycle of readings from our holy book, the lectionary. Even though the readings might sound familiar to us, Advent invites us to hear them in a new way. It has been three years since we last heard these readings. In that time we have changed. The world has changed. The church has changed. We need new ears in order to hear this Word on its own terms.

The sights around us change also. The secular world is probably already celebrating Christmas, missing altogether this somber season which invites us to look a little more closely into our own souls and then to look toward others, to see what presence of Jesus we might discover, "fresh in the flesh" this year.

On this first Sunday of Advent, why not try one of these suggestions as a way to make your own Advent time of preparation special:

1. Make an Advent wreath and/or light one candle and read the reflection.

2. Make a "shopping list" of the spiritual gifts you need.

3. Set a time to do your daily Advent reading and reflection.

4. Encourage someone else to observe Advent this year.

5. Check to see what your parish is doing to make Advent special.

6. Make a Jesse tree that celebrates the genealogy of Jesus. (A local religious goods store or your parish library may have books to help you with this.)

First Sunday
Year A

Isaiah 2:1–5 • Romans 13:11–14 • Matthew 24:37–44

A thin layer of ice hugs the shore of the pond these mornings. It is barely visible, but it is there. These cloudy, gray late-autumn days carelessly slip into the long darkness of the season. It is neither autumn nor winter. We are caught somewhere in between. Seagulls glean the remnant corn out of the nearby fields. Local clotheslines are festooned with the orange and camouflage colors of hunters. All around we see signs of nature's great annual turning in upon itself, looking for pockets of warmth and rest to endure yet another winter.

For believers, it is Advent. This season is so special. It is not so long, like Lent. Advent captures our imaginations. Advent is a little like that thin layer of ice: It is there, but not for long. Just as a few moments of sunshine melt away the ice, all kinds of influences vaporize Advent. Walk into any retail store in mid-September and you'll understand. Every year someone seems eager to steal our Advent, our holy season. That makes it harder to observe Advent, but maybe that makes it all the more special. People of faith are getting used to the world around us not understanding our season of preparation and stealing away that which is sacred.

We believers need to create for ourselves, for our churches, in our homes, and in our souls, an environment in which Advent can happen. Advent invites us to change—to look at ourselves, honestly, and to change. It summons us to face our doubts, our fears, our mistakes—all our personal darknesses—and to walk in that darkness trusting that Jesus is with us. Advent, you see, won't be intimidated. It returns year after year.

Advent begins with somber words: "Pay attention to the Lord!" "Pay attention to what God wants to do for us, through us, in us." That is what each reading commands this First Sunday of Advent. Some silence. Some darkness. A voice. Each week a little more light helps us to make our way through the darkness.

Advent is an attitude. Jesse trees and Advent wreaths help us to focus our attention on religion and not commercials. Isaiah and Matthew call to mind the words that count and not the words of clever ads. Advent insists that we see ourselves through different eyes, through God's vision of what the world should be and what we should be.

While the world rushes about carrying bundles of packages, we pause to let a single candle's flame remind us of what the season of gift-giving truly means. The world says the meaning of these weeks is economic recovery. We say it is recovering a sense of God and our Christian identity. The world says these weeks are for eating and drinking, but we hear Jesus say that "the coming of the Son of Man will repeat what happened in Noah's time when people were eating and drinking right up to the day Noah entered the ark." When we do what the rest of the world does, disaster follows.

Noah's neighbors were busy about their daily lives, and that is the problem. Like Noah's neighbors, we get so busy that we miss the larger patterns of life's purpose. We are just too busy. We watch TV. We watch for sales. We watch the time. Advent tells us to watch for Jesus, to see his presence in our world, in our spouse, in our children, in ourselves. We have a choice to make: to follow the easy way of Noah's neighbors, or to follow the gracious invitation of Isaiah to climb the Lord's mountain, to learn his ways, to turn from a way of life that is taking us breathless and worn-out to nowhere and, instead, to walk toward God.

"The Son of Man is coming at a time you least expect."

That is what Jesus says. We wait, not in fear, but in confidence and in hope. We take a careful look at ourselves and we let the magic of the season wrap around us, making us into a gift for God and for others. What do you watch for this Advent? What do you hope for this Advent? What gift do you need from God this year?

Questions for Reflection

1. Why does Advent slip away from us so easily?
2. Spend some time reflecting on the first reading. What actions are taking place in your world to deny its fulfillment? What signs are there of its fulfillment?
3. Paul wrote: "You know the time in which we are living." Is your outlook on our times and culture positive or negative? Why do you feel this way?
4. What change do you want to make this Advent?
5. How can you "pay attention to the Lord" this season when everything is so busy?

First Sunday
Year B

Isaiah 63:16–17, 19; 64:2–7 • 1 Corinthians 1:3–9
Mark 13:33–37

Autumn's darkness rests heavily upon us these days. Winter's annual death has hardened the ground. Heavier clothing reappears in our closets and wears heavy on our lives—the sad reminder of colder days to come. In the early morning a thin layer of ice coats the pond outside my window. The nip in the breeze forewarns us of winter's sting. Canadian geese, our honking visitors these last weeks, have gleaned the last of the corn from nearby fields and wisely made their way to warmer climes. Deepening shadows arrive earlier and earlier each day. Long darkness shrouds our world. A stillness beckons. Quiet. The world around us is settling in for the long season of waiting for rebirth.

Our inner clocks tease us into a new rhythm of life. We slow down. We gather warm blankets around us and sit in front of fireplaces, lulled into nodding sleep by lazy flames. We settle in for a long winter's nap.

The environment around us sends out the signal that it is time to slow down, to ease into a new, less stressful period of time. Such a tease! Everything human within us wants to cooperate with the great annual summons to slow the pace, to settle in, to rest. Other factors compete for our allegiance, however. Blaring television commercials and garish billboards remind us of another pattern of activity: the annual, frantic, breathless rush to prepare for yet another commercial Christmas, the victory of secular society over that which Christendom holds sacred.

The insistence of nature that we slow down competes with the ring of the cash register. Into the mix we add another message, another voice competing for our attention and for our loyalty. The gospel. The Word of God.

For Christians these deep days of early winter bring a strange gospel to our ears: "Be constantly on the watch! Stay awake!" Our comfort is disturbed. Our inner self is disquieted by these stark words. No quantity of Christmas cards, no amount of festive rush in the stores, not even the prospect of Jesus in the manger can hush the echo of the words uttered at the beginning of our Christian preparation for Christmas: "Stay awake! Be on guard!" It is Advent. Again.

The Advent season begins with the sober reminder of Our Lord's promise to come again—when we least expect him. It is Advent, the season of darkness. The dusks and midnights of our lives come into sharper focus. All this darkness—our anxieties, our fears, our faithlessness, our sin—begins to be dispelled by the fragile flame of a solitary candle light. There is hope.

Darkness may beckon us to slow down, but the shopkeeper's gospel urges us to get going. We who hear the gospel according to Mark this weekend are summoned to a different kind of attention—to holy wakefulness. We are called to choose between the frantic call of the marketplace and the sobering summons of Jesus, to choose between a season of nostalgia and a season of challenge. "What I say to you, I say to all: 'Be on guard!'" It is Advent. Again.

Questions for Reflection

1. What do you need to "watch out for" this Advent so that you won't get caught in all the busy activity of the season and forget its purpose?

2. What darkness is part of your life this year, a darkness that you look to God to brighten?

3. What darkness is around you, in family or friends, for which you can be light?

First Sunday
Year C

Jeremiah 33:14–16 • 1 Thessalonians 3:12–4:2
Luke 21:25–28, 34–36

It is Advent. Winter's darkness comes early and lasts through the long night. Crystalline air seems fragile, breakable. The early morning sun casts long shadows over the frost-covered lawn. Yesterday Caleb, my mini-dachshund pup, saw his shadow for the first time in that strange hour of day when night gives way to dawn. It confused him. At first he backed away from it, but his shadow stubbornly followed him around the yard. His confusion yielded to bravado, and he tried to bark it away, but the shadow would not be cowed. Finally he made his peace with reality.

Advent is like that long, morning shadow. It confuses us. Or perhaps it just confuses the world around us, the unbelieving world. It is a troubled season. It is troubled because, like a shadow, it is elusive. It is there, but the world tries to back away from it, to cover it over with tinsel and baubles. The world also tries to outshout its prophetic voices, to bark it away with countless holiday celebrations before December 25th. But Advent won't be intimidated. We need to make our peace with it. To observe it. To cherish it.

Week after week we gather in our parish churches to hear the Word of God. We listen to it tugging at our souls, our minds, our very selves. It invites, cajoles, begs, demands, and teases us into seeing a kingdom of God which is bigger and more glorious, more noble, and more enduring than this passing world of ours. That is why our first Advent reflection comes from these powerful words of Luke: "People will die of fright in anticipation of what is coming upon the earth." Those who don't listen need to fear.

Advent begins a new time of listening to this Word of God, a new season of grace, a new year of hope. Advent begins a listening to the same words we have heard before, some of them many times. Yet we hear them differently because we have changed since the last time we heard them. Our parishes have changed, our church has changed, and the world in which we live has also changed since the last time we heard these readings.

Change is a marvelous testimony to the success of Advent. The clarion call of the Advent prophets is "Change," to change ourselves over and over again as we prepare to discern the places in our lives and our church where we find Jesus, the Word always becoming flesh in us.

This Advent we begin a year of gospels from the pen and faith of Luke. It is a year of sharing the faith and experience of Christians from faraway places and long-ago times, Christians who waited for the Lord's return. How surprised they would be to see us still waiting.

Advent always begins with the startling summons to shape up because we never know when the Lord will return. In this reading from Luke's gospel Jesus issues two serious commandments: "Be on guard! Pray constantly!"

This first Advent gospel sobers us into the realization that our preparation for Christmas should not only focus on gifts and decorations and on what happened long ago in Bethlehem. This is a safe and familiar reflection. This gospel reminds us that Advent actually prepares us for the Lord's glorious Second Coming, the unknown future, the realm of faith in God's power and God's goodness.

For those who don't believe, faith is the realm of shadows. For those of us who do believe, Advent may mean days of deep darkness, but with the prophets we see the

Light who is coming into our lives. We take time to reflect on those parts of our lives that cry out for the love and presence of the Savior. You see, the prophets are correct. "The days are coming" when there will be no more darkness, no more shadows. During this season we make our peace with Jesus who never really left us, who is always coming into our lives.

Questions for Reflection

1. What is confusing you this year about your life—what needs attention and time—and how can you do something about it instead of just hoping it will go away?

2. What are you afraid of—and how does it reveal your lack of faith—or a misunderstanding about God?

3. The readings warn us to "pray constantly." What time can you reserve each day for these reflections? When can you find time to get closer to God before Christmas?

Monday of the First Week

Isaiah 2:1–5 • Psalm 122 • Matthew 8:5–11

Few words ever written have inspired as many people as have Isaiah's words about turning swords into plowshares. As this year's Advent slowly emerges from the shadows of winter's darkness, the prophet calls us to an incredible, almost unbelievable, vision of what our world can be like when God is truly with us, and when we allow ourselves to be truly with God.

The setting is the New Jerusalem, the kingdom yet to come. Isaiah would be astonished to know that people are still waiting for this vision to come to pass. I think he would be pleased to see the faith of people, hoping for the same thing that he hoped for: trust in God's Word to save us. Trust in God's Word to set things right. Trust in the unique combination of divine summons and human response.

The unity of peoples and nations for which we yearn seems to become tangible at this time of year, even if just for a fleeting moment. Isaiah offers that vision not just for us, but for all people, Gentile and Jew. All will come to Zion, to Jerusalem, to hear the sacred word that can make it all happen.

Jesus knew that word. Just like Isaiah of old, he spoke its promise to Gentile and to Jew. It is fitting that this first Advent weekday gospel offers God's promise and salvation to the whole world. In Jesus' time many Jews were awaiting a messiah, a savior, but like most of us, they looked for salvation in strange places and then wondered why their hope was disappointed. In this gospel, a foreigner, a pagan, a member of the anonymous multitude of nations, believes in Jesus when others don't.

In the darkness of this Advent morning we are given a

deep mystery to ponder: God's ineffable, powerful Word at work from the beginning of creation, calling the world into existence, sustaining it, guiding it, challenging it, challenging us. Each word of today's readings could be its own homily, a retreat on the promises God makes to us and on our choices to believe in those promises. Today that word is clearly offered not just to us, who think we deserve it, but to all—especially those we most likely despise. All of us need this word. Some will listen, like the centurion.

Today we share the eucharist. Later all will share the banquet of heaven, the bounty of faith, the same faith of Abraham, Isaac, and Jacob. Some will use this day, this Advent, to let the splendid vision of peace pass into their souls. "O house of Jacob, come, let us walk in the light of the Lord." What a wonderful prayer to begin our Advent. In the darkest moments of winter, the prophet issues an invitation to warmth, to light, to make a home for God in our lives, to come home to God.

Prayer
Lord God, throughout the ages you have called people to yourself. As I begin this new Advent you are calling me to stretch my soul and climb a mountain, the mountain that leads to your presence, to seeing you more clearly in my life, in my neighbor, and in my world. Give me the strength and discipline I need to be faithful to you and to this season of quiet prayer. I ask this through Jesus, our Lord, who is coming into my life in new ways this season. Amen.

Tuesday of the First Week

Isaiah 11:1–10 • Psalm 72 • Luke 10:21–24

A favorite Advent song is "Savior of the Nations, Come." It is gentle and melodic. In words and music it summarizes the theology of this season: longing for the presence of the Savior.

Today the prophet Isaiah reminds us of the importance of genealogy, the origins of the Messiah. Luke reminds us of the good fortune that is ours as believers: We have seen the Savior that the nations longed to see. We are more fortunate than kings and prophets.

Twice Isaiah reminds us that a day is coming that will involve wonderful actions from the family tree of Jesse, the father of King David. How appropriate that this poem from Isaiah speaks about the need for justice. Justice was the work of the king in ancient Israel. When the king acted with proper judgment, all would be well for the nation. By the time of Isaiah, however, the people of Israel and Judah had known generations of abusive and faithless kings. All of these "messiahs" brought disaster to the nation. They longed for a king who would work for justice and be energetic about the kingdom of God.

The result of this justice would be peace. All nature would return to the harmonious coexistence of Paradise if only the king would act justly. So wonderful would life be in Israel that all the surrounding nations would recognize God as the origin of this wonderful harmony. They would seek the God who made such a life possible.

In today's gospel we overhear a private conversation between Jesus and his disciples. Jesus was the long-awaited one whose death and resurrection, whose preaching and example, would bring that oft-promised justice and peace to anyone who sought it. The prophets of old could only dream about it. Kings with all their worldly power could not muster the kingdom of God into existence. Only Jesus can do that.

In the early days of Advent we set the pace for the rest of the season. We utter an earnest prayer for justice and peace in our own lives, in our church, in our nation. "Savior of the Nations, Come!" Unite us to the family tree of faithful people, the root of Jesse, who eagerly await your return and who quietly pause to pray that this vision of Isaiah will come to fulfillment.

Prayer

Lord God, you always were and always will be. Sometimes it is hard, though, to see you now. These readings show that you do work in history and in human families, with all their foibles and all their potential. Help me today to see my role in your plan, to understand better that all those other people around me are part of your family, too, and that we all wait together for the "Savior of the Nations" to come. Help me to wait today with prayer and patience. Amen.

Wednesday of the First Week

Isaiah 25:6–10 • Psalm 23 • Matthew 15:29–37

On the northern shore of the Sea of Galilee the German Benedictine monks are the guardians of a beautiful church which marks the site of the multiplication of the loaves and fish. This is the same Sea of Galilee that we read about in today's gospel. The same waves gently, lazily wash against the shore. Here, on the bluffs of the shoreline, people have rested and wondered and dreamed. The site is close to the town Jesus chose as his own homeplace, Capharnaum. It is not difficult to imagine the people of that town walking ten minutes to the solitude of the beach to get away from the bustle of the busy fishing village and its noisy caravans and ever-present Roman soldiers.

Today's gospel tells us that one day Jesus came here and large crowds of people followed him. Those who followed were heroic, for they were sick, crippled, blind, and mute. They were the assembly of those God had seemed to forget. For some time now Jesus has been feeding them with words and with hope. But when push came to shove, it was more than words that these people needed. They needed healing and Jesus healed them. They also needed bread, nourishment for the day. And Jesus provided it for them.

Isaiah's prophecy speaks about the day of the messiah, the magnificent time when this people that seldom had much to eat, much less the best cuisine, would share the messianic banquet of God's kingdom. When the messiah came, they would have plenty of food and drink, the choicest steaks and vintage wine. Unparalleled rejoicing at God's goodness would characterize their spirit.

Matthew shows us that Jesus fulfilled this expectation. The early church clearly saw the prophecy of Isaiah, spoken so long ago, come to fulfillment in Jesus, come to fulfillment for them. When they gathered to celebrate the breaking of the bread in their early liturgies they remembered Isaiah's words and they recalled the actions of Jesus. They recognized that somehow they shared in the messianic presence of Jesus. They kept alive his healing touch, his concern for the crowds who were lost. They continued to break bread with one another in memory of him.

Advent reminds us that just waiting for the Messiah to return is not enough. We are that messianic people who bring the presence of Christ into the world. That must be part of our Advent spirituality, our preparation for Christmas.

At Tabgha, the Benedictine monastery on the shore of Galilee, monks and lay volunteers still break the bread of the Eucharist in a splendid but simple basilica built on this historic site. But they don't stop there. They have learned well the lesson of these readings. They conduct a camp in this beautiful place for Jewish, Muslim, and Christian children and adults whose lives are less fortunate than most. Here, on the slopes of the shoreline, they gather the mute, the lame, the blind, the sick, all those fragments of human life that God wishes to touch through human hands and believing hearts. The promise of Isaiah and the fulfilling action of Jesus still takes place along the Sea of Galilee.

Prayer
Jesus, it seems so easy to picture you in Galilee doing your marvels, speaking your words, gathering the hurting to yourself. Open my eyes to see the needs of those around me, my neighbors, family, and friends. Help me to use my resources of time and talent to make you part of their lives. Then I will be able to see you more clearly in my own life. Amen.

Thursday of the First Week

Isaiah 26:1–6 • Psalm 118 • Matthew 7:21, 24–27

The Old City of Jerusalem stands proud on the ancient rock scarp upon which an unknown people built its first habitations long before history was recorded. Successive waves of people, conquerors, and new conquerors have always rebuilt this "Foundation of Peace, " this Jerusalem, on this same place.

Visitors to Jerusalem today see the wall built in the 1500s to protect the citizens from invaders. Some fifty feet high and two-and-a-half miles in circumference, the massive rock wall is a symbol of this city's pride and endurance. Presently seven gates lead into the city. An eighth gate was walled shut when a Moslem caliph heard that the Jewish messiah was to enter through it. By blocking its entry, he attempted to foil the plan of God.

The seven open gates bear the scars of centuries of warfare. Bullets have pockmarked each wall which stands as a mute witness to the need for such protection. In former days the gates were closed and barred at night. An enemy would have a hard time entering. So would any citizen who stayed out past curfew!

"Open the gates to let in a nation that is just!" That is the command of Isaiah. "Let in the nation that keeps peace." The strength of the city depended upon its external protection and its internal integrity. The prophets were both practical and hopeful. The gates would keep out enemies, but they also allowed the faithful to enter.

In today's Advent reflection Isaiah offers us the chance to come to God, to come into Jerusalem, the holy city of God. The ramparts and defenses will keep out the riff-raff. Good walls, like good fences, see to that.

The latecomers could cry all night for entrance, but no

one would open the gates for them. In the gospel, Matthew warns us of the same thing. Latecomers, those unknown to Jesus, will come seeking entrance into the kingdom of God. "Lord, Lord" they will shout, but shouting doesn't impress Jesus.

This Advent gospel reminds us of an important truth about shouting and noise. All the noise of this busy season doesn't impress God. One thing only matters: how we live God's Word. Do we let the Word of God encircle our lives and everything we do?

The key needed to enter the gates of heaven is the Word of God. Advent is a time when we prepare for the Incarnation, when the eternal Word of God takes on human flesh. In this Advent we are offered the chance to enter the kingdom by taking the words of Jesus seriously, by unlocking the stone-cold doors of our bitter and frustrated and faithless hearts. Advent is the time to break down the walls we build in our relationships. It is time to let the words we have been hearing take on some flesh of their own by the way we put them into practice.

Prayer

Lord God, we build so many walls in our lives, walls that keep other people distant from our lives and walls that we think hide us from you. Help us to use this Advent weekday to discover what walls you are looking to dismantle. Help us to see today what barriers we place between ourselves and others. Help us to open the gates to our hearts and make ourselves into our Advent gift to you. Amen.

Friday of the First Week

Isaiah 29:17–24 • Psalm 27 • Matthew 9:27–31

Lebanon has been in the news often over the past few years. The word from there has seldom been good. Years ago its capital, Beirut, was called the "Paris of the Middle East." Now it is a by-word for destruction.

Isaiah foresees a happier Lebanon. He sees life-giving orchards and forested land bringing life and beauty to the countryside. He also sees other things more deeply than most people. As a prophet, he sees things the way God sees them: in the future.

In today's passage from the Hebrew Scriptures (Old Testament) he sees a time when the blind will see, the deaf will hear, and the poor will have a reason to rejoice. That was hardly the day-to-day situation in his time. In his vision he sees wandering, lost people finding their way back to God. Such a future!

In the gospel we encounter Jesus with two blind men who seem bent on making a nuisance of themselves. They chase after Jesus, in their blind way taking some time to catch up with him. Isn't that the way it often is for us: We chase after Jesus, stumbling along the way?

I suspect they came two-by-two because alone they would have been too afraid. Sometimes we need other people. There is a wisdom in recognizing when. Notice that Jesus didn't stop to let them catch up to him. He just kept going to his destination, to the house, to the place where faithful people gather around Jesus.

Once they reach Jesus they make their request. Our gospel doesn't tell us if they were bold or nervous. We simply learn that they ask for the one thing they need most: the healing gift of sight. The first comment that Jesus makes to them is a question: "Are you confident that I can do this?"

Jesus doesn't ask them about their medical condition or how long they have been blind. He doesn't ask for any credentials.

They have made their way through the uneven paths of ancient Palestine, no easy accomplishment. They went through this trouble because all along they had trust in Jesus. They had the confidence in his power and his goodness that is the prerequisite for God's help. It was faith that healed them. That same faith heals people today.

The prophet Isaiah had spoken before about "the coming days" when the blind would see. Now these two anonymous men have received the gift of sight. To our gospel writer, this was a clear sign that the messiah was finally present among his people, fulfilling all those marvelous expectations of Isaiah. Jesus performed the marvels that the Messiah was expected to accomplish. Truly, Jesus was the Messiah. Advent had arrived.

In our own time Lebanon has become a by-word for destruction and violence. It awaits the redeeming touch of God that will again bring peace and restore its beauty. We also wait in our time for the redeeming, healing touch of God in our national lives, to end the problems that beset our nation. God also redeems our personal lives, giving us the wonderful gift of insight, that is, true sight to see the powerful presence of God ever among us.

Prayer
Seeing. Such a simple and common part of our daily lives. How we take sight for granted. Help us today, Jesus, to open our eyes to see with our hearts and our souls and not just our eyes. Help us today to see you in others and to see your power in the world around us, calling us to use all these signs to find our way to you. "Lord, that we might see." Amen.

Saturday of the First Week

Isaiah 30:19–21; 23–26 • Psalm 147
Matthew 9:35—10:1,6–8

Teaching is hard work. A good teacher stays current in the field, updates class notes and methods, and is concerned that students learn the significance of the material rather than just the factual information. We all remember good teachers and bad ones. Good teachers had a way of making us want to be like them, to follow in their footsteps.

Isaiah knew about teachers. He was probably a teacher himself, one of the educated wise men who worked in the royal palace, giving instruction to the scions of noble families and to future kings. Good education, even then, was like food for the mind, another kind of daily bread that we need to be truly human.

A good teacher shows us the way to proceed through life. Following certain steps and procedures will lead to success. Deviation from them can lead to disaster. In today's reading a marvelous promise is made: God himself will be our teacher. No substitutes or lesser qualified candidates need apply. God will give instruction about the way he has chosen for us. God will teach us the lessons we need to know for life, not with threats and blows, but by gently encouraging us. "This is the way. Walk in it." When we lean too far to the left or the right and begin to topple over, God's instruction will straighten us out.

Jesus understands this. He is a master-teacher himself. Most of his time is spent teaching people who have forgotten how to walk with God. Toward God. In today's passage we meet Jesus teaching people in the synagogue. He is teaching crowds of people, not just a disciple here or there. Again the prophecy of Isaiah is coming true: God is teaching his people. The teacher of righteousness is present, bringing the people to understand their own dignity and goodness.

Jesus accomplishes the goal of all good teachers: to make disciples in their own image and likeness. Those who have been closest to Jesus, listening most attentively, are given a share in the power and work and ministry of their teacher. Jesus sends them out to begin their time of apprenticeship.

The community always shares responsiblity for what it has learned and seeks to pass it on to others. "The gift you have received, give as a gift." Those are the words of Jesus. In this season which gets so easily preoccupied with buying and giving and receiving gifts, the gospel reminds us that only one gift counts—the gift of faith. It is to be given generously and freely.

Prayer
Lord God, you teach by word and by example. Help us to listen more attentively to your word, both in worship and in private prayer. Help us to see in the lives of those around us your mysterious, hidden presence, always teaching a little more about what it means to be faithful, to be baptized. Let this day be spent opening our eyes and ears to all the ways you lead us closer to you. And let our own example be a good teacher for others. Amen.

The Second Week of Advent

Every year, no matter which cycle of the lectionary we read, the liturgy for the Second Sunday of Advent invites us to do two things:

1. to go into the desert of Judea, and
2. to listen to the voice of John the Baptizer.

Our own image of the Baptizer usually derives from picture books. John is bearded and wears rough clothing. The bible tells us that his clothing was this simple. So was his diet. How odd that people would travel many miles to see him and, in most cases, to be insulted by him. Like the prophets of old, his words were aimed at effect, not politeness. He cut to the very center of people's lives, demanding that they shape up their souls.

As this Second Week of Advent enters our lives, here are some suggestions to help make the time pass in harmony with the spirit of the season.

1. Light the second candle of the Advent wreath in addition to the first one.

2. Check how well you are doing with your daily meditation. If you've slipped, that's okay. This week you can do better.

3. What would John the Baptizer say directly to you? to your family? to your parish?

4. The crowds went to the desert to hear John. These days the crowds are going to the malls to shop. Find a place, if possible away from home, where you can go just to sit and ponder the power of John's words and what they offer to you.

Second Sunday
Year A

Isaiah 11:1–10 • Romans 15:4–9 • Matthew 3:1–12

It is the season of darkest winter. The brief day quickly melts into an early and long night. Fireplaces are lit early, electric lights burn throughout our homes, and here and there, a second Advent candle pierces the darkness of our souls, bringing God's light into our world, slowly bringing the light of the world, Jesus, into our lives.

This Second Sunday of Advent bids us to travel again, to move from our comfortable habitats and habits into the un-comfortable region of Judea's wilderness—and of our own souls. Advent, you see, is a tough taskmaster. Advent won't let us settle in or get too comfortable.

Our journey takes us away from the familiar patterns of life and into the wilderness. The desert. For some reason God seems to favor this place. God revealed life and love to Moses and the Hebrews in the desert, sustained Elijah in the wilderness, and saves, perhaps, some surprising revelation for us in this place, in this season.

We go to hear John the Baptizer. Once this man attracted crowds of people. Now he summons us and so we go to the desert, to its edge, to the shores of the Jordan River. Tradition marks the inglorious spot where John preached. The Jordan slugs its crooked way through the valley formed millions of years ago. Along its path, there is veg-etation. Wherever people have planted seed, its water gives life. But the place to which we go is not a resort. It is desert. Dry. Most of the year the shoreline is a dust bowl. Pilgrims raise little storm clouds of dust as they trudge along. It is like walking on the moon. In the rainy season, it is worse. The mud shows no favorites. All get messy from the journey. It is not easy to go to see John. Nor is it easy to hear his words, for he looks into our eyes, sees our souls, talks to our sinfulness, and commands it to leave us, to make some room for a change, for a messiah, for Jesus.

John is, by anyone's reckoning, a strange fellow. The circumstances of his unusual conception and birth give a mythic quality to the early life of this curious stranger who stands in water and mud, who eats grasshoppers, who dresses in camel-hair clothing, and who has the nerve to tell us to change.

"Reform your lives!" "Prepare the way of the Lord!" That is his message. Simple, direct, blunt. Prepare! This is a season of preparation, isn't it? Everyone is a little busier than normal these days, aren't they? Buying this, ordering that, fixing this, decorating that, making this, wrapping that, going here, then going there. What a strange litany!

Then along comes John. And his message. He tells us that it is okay to be a little selfish during this season. What a strange thing to say in the season of giving! But it is true. John says it is okay to pull back from all this holiday hoopla. He tells us that reforming our lives is more important than re-shaping the branches of the Christmas tree. John tells us that fixing ourselves, our relationships to God and others, is more important than fixing broken things. John commands us to repair ourselves and to prepare our lives because the first and foremost gift that we give is ourselves.

Like the curious crowd that went out to see John, we might get a little dusty and muddy in our effort to reform. We might even get a little lost on the way to find our souls, but John's voice is loud and clear and it will direct our efforts and direct us to God. Listen again: "Reform your lives." Reshape your lives: your attitudes, your actions, your behavior. There are some twenty shopping days left until Christmas, so says the world. But for us, the days are filled with the haunting voice of John, calling to us to reform our lives, to prepare the way of the Lord, and to make straight God's paths by straightening out our lives.

Questions for Reflection

1. What does it mean "to go into the desert"?

2. What preparation for the real meaning of Christmas do you need to make this week? How can you find time to do it?

3. What parts of your life need re-shaping by God this season? What are the signs of God's activity working in you right now? Are you resisting them?

Second Sunday
Year B

Isaiah 40:1–5, 9–11 • 2 Peter 3:8–14 • Mark 1:1–8

Shhhh. Quiet. Listen. The sounds echo off the steep walls of the valley. What sounds are these, these hushed whispers of the crowd? Peasant plaincloth and regal purple meld together into a strange rainbow as both pass through the valley, descending, always descending. Some are moving into the depths of their own souls. Others merely descend the steep, dusty grade that leads from Jerusalem to the mysterious, eerie wilderness of Judah.

It is only a half-day's walk from Jerusalem, going downhill. Ancient knapsacks are packed with sandwiches. Goatskins are filled with spring water, renewed by the occasional lush waterfalls that grace the valley known as Wadi Qelt.

The steady tread of these wilderness pilgrims beats a strange tattoo into the hillsides. Birds, goats, and gazelles peer from afar, wondering what these people are doing in their territory. Wondering where they are going. The low murmur of the throng is a quiet chorus of questions: Who is he? Where did he come from? What is he like? Is he a revolutionary? Why are we going to hear him? What will he say today? Is he Elijah returned to us? Could it be that the messiah is truly coming? Is he the messiah? Such questions!

Among the hikers that day, perhaps there is an itinerant rabbi from Nazareth. You know, the carpenter's son. All of them going through the valley to the wilderness where the Jordan is.

The pilgrims march on to an encounter with the man of God, a man as strange as this season of Advent. In this season the measured seriousness of the Baptizer's words clashes with the festive shouts of the shopkeeper's gospels. The charismatic figure of John the Baptizer dominates our Advent liturgies. This week and next the church spotlights this man of powerful words, the precursor of the Christ. He is an anomaly now as he was then. People who go about in hairy costumes telling us that we ought to repent because the reign of God is near don't easily measure up to our notions of Christianity American-style. His presence today in our churches would be an embarrassment like the bugs that surely romped about in his camel-hair clothing.

The message of this man of God beckoned crowds of people to leave their own forms of comfort and to seek God in the wilderness. Can we leave the comfort of our religiosity and seek God in the wilderness of our own souls?

The haunting voice of this desert man cannot be tamed. Herod Antipas tried to silence truth by cutting off the Baptizer's head. But here we are, in Advent nearly two thousand years later, still hearing his voice. What a strange voice! John calls us to look at ourselves, acknowledge our sins, and change.

He asks hard, penetrating questions: Are you at peace with yourself? with others? with God? If not, then come to the desert and hear my voice! Do you live with many pressures, too busy to pray? Then take the time to come into my Advent-desert and hear my voice! Has routine robbed you of a certain joy for living? Then come to the desert and hear my voice! I want to tell you that God is here, with us. Believe it!

In the first reading, mountains and valleys are the obstacles to God. For John, selfishness and sin are the obstacles. Often we create our own obstacles. But now it is Advent, time to "make ready the way of the Lord, to clear him a straight path."

We join the pilgrims who make their way into the desert, down to the Jordan to hear a voice of faith that resounds through the ages. We respond to the voice that summons us to honest self-evaluation, to change our ways, and to let the water of our own baptism wash over us again.

Questions for Reflection

1. Where would John the Baptizer preach today—what setting would he choose?

2. John the Baptizer summoned people out of their comfortable lives into the desert. What part of your religious life has become too comfortable, in need of challenge?

3. What do you need to do to be at peace with God? with yourself?

Second Sunday
Year C

Baruch 5:1–9 • Philippians 1:4-6, 8–11 • Luke 3:1–6

It is still Advent. Our winter darkness is accented by blustery winds and snowfalls that turn our plans inside out. When the world around us is snow-filled and cold it is difficult to turn our minds to a gospel that carries us into a distant, unseen, dry desert. We cannot fight the gospel, however, even though we try. Sooner or later, inevitably, the gospel wins. That is the lesson of this Advent Sunday. But will we learn it?

Our destination is the wilderness of Judea, that vast area of hills and depressions south and east of Jerusalem. It sweeps over the landscape, mocking efforts throughout the ages to build roads or to harvest crops. There the earth is dry, parched like a soul without God. Most of the year little dust storms form wherever people or animals set foot. It is not a pleasant place. But it is a special one.

Throughout Israel's long history unusual events have taken place in this setting. It is no surprise that John the Baptizer is here. All the religious fanatics begin here. Why should John be an exception? In this fragile area where the Jordan River snakes through the earth, bringing life and refreshment, John sets up his headquarters. The Essenes, those mystics who recorded the Dead Sea Scrolls, live nearby. Perhaps they have provided John with hospitality or food for thought. Jericho is nearby, too. Its ancient glory lies covered by the dust of the centuries. In John's time a newer city, filled with soldiers and aristocrats, had usurped Jericho's place along the river.

A long time ago Moses led people through water, from slavery to freedom, from death to life. Joshua then brought the descendents of those people across the Jordan's waters, mimicking the actions of Moses. When the people of Jerusalem were taken into exile, their last view of the Promised Land was this river and the wilderness beyond it that led back to their homes. It was also their first view when returning. This is the setting that Luke pictures for us in today's gospel.

Centuries before, the anonymous prophet known to us as "Second Isaiah" spoke about a glorious homecoming from exile and a return to Jerusalem. These same barren wastes offered safety, the way home. This difficult terrain would be leveled, making an easy path for his worn-out people to return. There would be a glorious procession of faithful, purified people making their way back to Jerusalem, making their way back home, to God.

At first it seems strange that John chose the desert to make his announcement, to proclaim that Isaiah's prophecy was coming true in new ways. John did not choose to preach in the centers of political or religious power. He chose the desert. He knew his history. He knew his theology. Centuries before, Isaiah promised that God would comfort his people in this place. Now John announced a new kind of prophecy: God will comfort his people in ways they never imagined. The geographic exile in Babylon was a great trauma, but it is nothing compared to the soul's exile from God. The journey home from Babylon was long and uncomfortable. Ask anyone who has ever trekked through this wilderness. The spiritual journey back to God can be even more significant, and often more difficult.

John the Baptizer announced the Advent of God's Word. It was powerfully present in the political and religious world of his time, as it is in our own times as well. How far are we from God as a nation? as a parish? as a family? as an individual? In what wilderness of the soul do we wander? How rough is the way back to God for us during these remaining days of Advent? John offers us the refreshing water of the Jordan to revive our tired spirits. John offers us the forgiveness of sins to prepare the way for the Holy One. John offers us the chance to see God's will for us.

He is a strange one, this John the Baptizer. His voice is like an alarm clock, startling us out of a comfortable winter sleep. He dwells where other people fear to go. He dwells in the wilderness of our own souls, challenging us to make an Advent's journey back to God, to straighten out our twisted thinking about God and neighbor, to smooth out the rough relationships that could make Christmas awkward. He challenges us to admit that there is room in our lives for a Savior, and for Advent.

Questions for Reflection

1. John the Baptizer startled people with his ways and his message. What surprise can you arrange for yourself or your family or a friend to show that something new is happening in your life?

2. Is there a place you can make into your own "desert" for a little while during Advent, a place for escape, in order to break the routine of your life?

3. Whose voice or ideas or challenges might be speaking to you this Advent, asking you to grow up a little more in faith? How do you listen to this voice?

Monday of the Second Week

Isaiah 35:1–10 • Psalm 85 • Luke 5:17–26

Advent is the time of the year that marks the beginning of winter for the northern hemisphere. Even in faraway Israel, it is winter. There, winter means cooler, but not cold, temperatures. It also means rain, the life-giving rain that drenches the land for these few months of the year, preparing it for the long summer drought.

At the first rainfall the people of Israel do not scurry for shelter. Instead they stand out in the refreshing rain and comment one to another about the reality of the weather. Not far from Jerusalem, where the Judean wilderness stretches across the landscape, the rains give life to seeds that have lain hidden within the soil these many months. Literally overnight the desert areas turn green and flowers blossom. Sometimes there are traffic jams as people rush out to see the spectacle!

Only God can be responsible for such a marvel, for such life-giving grace. Isaiah knew this. He believed it. So he wrote about it for people who were beginning to lose faith in God's power to help them. In today's reading Isaiah offers an eloquent poem about God changing nature: Where once there was desert, now there is tillable soil. Where once there was drought, now there are streams bursting their banks. Where people were weak and feeble in limb and timid of heart, there will be strength. This is the work that God will do for his people.

The gospel offers us a glimpse into the fulfillment of Isaiah's promise. Advent follows that pattern: promise and fulfillment. The fulfillment is the presence of Jesus going about curing illness, changing weak limbs into strong bodies, timid followers into courageous disciples, and vascillating faith into boldness for the sake of the kingdom of God.

Today's gospel offers us a broad spectrum of such characteristics. The leaders of the people who should have been filled with faith are filled only with doubt and a certain self-satisfied religious snobbery. The poor paralyzed man did not have access to Jesus, but he had friends: a community that helped him to find Jesus, to find a cure, to find salvation. No one can do it alone. We need a community of believers to help us find our way to the Lord.

The recipient of God's grace in the gospel is nameless. I find it curiously touching that he never even speaks to Jesus. It was stubborn faith and the will of his friends that made the difference. The only words the paralytic speaks are at the end of the episode. He praises God. And then the fickle crowd follows his lead. The man who could lead no one because of a physical paralysis becomes a leader in spiritual matters. Everyone praises God! "We have seen incredible things today!"

We see incredible things in our times as well. From space exploration to medical technology, marvelous events are almost commonplace in our lives. But one thing remains special: Jesus. And the people who believe in him and who help others find their way to the Lord.

Prayer
Lord God, rain seems like such an ordinary thing, but to those who live without it, it is a grace. So much of my life seem ordinary too, so ordinary that sometimes I forget to see what a blessing the routine of each day can be. The paralyzed man needed help, and so do I. That man needed your help and the help of those who loved him. Today, help me to see through the ordinary events and the regular people that are part of my day, and help me to see how I can bring someone closer to you. Amen.

Tuesday of the Second Week

Isaiah 40:1–11 • Psalm 96 • Matthew 18:12–14

I had the opportunity to live in Israel for several years. During that time I absorbed the sights, sounds, and smells of a culture that is as new as today's dawn and as ancient as the first sunrise.

In that land many of the inhabitants are shepherds, exactly as we read in the bible. This is not the large cattle industry of our American West. Rather, it is the life of the small rural village where many families tend their flocks in the nearby hills.

Shepherds get mixed publicity in that place. We tend to look at them through the romantic eyes of artists. "I am the Good Shepherd" comes immediately to mind. In truth, the life of the shepherd was often nothing more than a dull and boring routine. The only excitement came when a wild animal threatened the flock. In biblical times shepherds were often looked down upon as a scruffy, rascally bunch who didn't keep the law. They were more likely to steal a sheep than to care for it.

In that setting, the question of Jesus in today's gospel is remarkable. "What is your thought on this?" he asks. The truth of the matter is that no shepherd would risk danger to the other ninety-nine sheep in order to search for one foolish stray. No shepherd would take the chance that he'd lose all in order to find one. No human shepherd, that is. The point of the gospel becomes clear. God is no ordinary shepherd. Once again the words of Isaiah come to pass: "Like a shepherd he feeds his flock and in his arms he gathers the lambs." The prophecy is a remarkable insight into the God whose ways are different from our human ways. So different that God will send his Son to be the Savior, to show us how to shepherd one another.

Many times it may seem that we are lost as we make our way through life. Sometimes it seems that God has forgotten to look for us. But then we hear these Advent readings and we are reminded that it is our thinking that is a bit mixed up. God is always searching for us, especially in the darkness of our Advent souls.

Prayer
Lord God, how often I feel like a lost sheep, like someone in need of guidance. What a comfort to hear the reassuring words of the prophet, that you yourself will take care of me, better than any politician, better than any person could imagine. I know that I, too, have a responsibility to search out the lost, to try to be a leader by my own example. Help me to trust your words and your ways. Help me to place myself in your care and then to help others find their way home to you by my example. Help me to see the special way that you are bringing me closer to you this Advent. Amen.

Wednesday of the Second Week

Isaiah 40:25–31 • Psalm 103 • Matthew 11:28–30

For us who were born into Christian families and for almost anyone living in North America today, it is quite impossible to imagine the religious lives of the people who first heard Isaiah's prophecy. Much of the bible focuses on the choices these people had to make about God. In biblical times, especially during the times recorded in the Hebrew Scriptures, people honored many, many gods. A god might have power over only a certain territory, like Canaan or Egypt, but the people certainly believed in many gods.

Often the Chosen People were influenced by the beliefs of their neighbors and strayed from their belief in Yahweh, the one true God. The question in those times was never the existence of God. There was no such thing as atheism. The great theological questions were, "Who is our god?" and "What do we have to do to keep this god off our backs?"

Centuries of living with God, obeying and disobeying the commandments, and experiencing God's activity in history had to take place before the people of Israel were totally convinced that not only was their God, Yahweh, on their side, but that in fact only Yahweh was God. All others were less than false. They were nothing.

In that context God's question, as related in Isaiah, makes sense: "To whom can you liken me as an equal?" The answer is, of course, "No one." God is unique. No image is adequate to capture all that it is to be God.

The eternal sovereign Lord of history is filled with vitality, all of which is used on behalf of his weary people. God's people, you see, were experiencing the rigors of life in exile. They had lost a great war with Babylon and were living as refugees in a land where foreign gods dominated politics and religion. During these sad times some of the greatest literature and growth in religious thinking took place. This passage from Isaiah is an example of that.

In the years that Jesus lived on this earth, the fortunes of God's people had again turned sour. Foreign power occupied the land. Rome's all-powerful hand seemed too strong for any human opposition. Life was burdensome and dangerous. All of life's normal difficulties—lack of money, unemployment, sickness—were made worse by the hopeless situation of the times.

To these people Jesus speaks a word of consolation. To follow him does not mean additional burdens, it means joy. There is no cost. His way, which is God's way, liberates people from the toil and cares that sap their energies.

As Advent makes deeper inroads into our own daily lives we are given the chance to learn in a few days time what took centuries for others to comprehend: God does not want life to be unhappy or problematic. God's will is for us joyfully to acknowledge that reality and that care for each of us. In the darkness of our own problems the Advent light of Jesus comes with its beauty and simplicity. "Learn from me, for I am gentle and humble of heart."

Prayer
Lord God, there are many ideas and many things that compete for my loyalty. My own use of time and the money I spend reveal how many "gods" there can be in my life. Let me see that you alone are truly God, that nothing, no-thing, can compare to you. Show me how to focus my attention and love on revealing your goodness to others. In the over-decorated, frantically busy, and under-spiritualized world around me, let the simplicity and humility of your Son be reflected in my example and in my home. Amen.

Thursday of the Second Week

Isaiah 41:13–20 • Psalm 145 • Matthew 11:11–15

Throughout the gospels Jesus has encouraging words for those who are wise enough to listen, and sharp words for those whose hearts are hard and whose ears are closed. Often Jesus' words of encouragement are given to anonymous beneficiaries. We seldom learn of their fates after meeting Jesus. We only know that somehow the Holy Spirit filled them with enough courage and faith to come forward and encounter the Messiah.

The sharpest rebukes of Jesus are reserved for the learned and the powerful, for those people who should be able to make a difference in people's lives, those who should lead the way. Throughout the pages of the bible most of these powerful people are shown for what they are: clay-footed, hard-hearted, soul-less aristocrats and opportunists. Jesus has no time for such as these.

We should pay special attention, then, when Jesus does offer compliments to people. In today's gospel he heaps praises upon his famous cousin, the desert-dwelling baptizer, John. The evangelists have Jesus stating clearly that no one who ever lived was more important than John: "I solemnly assure you, history has not known a man born of woman greater than John the Baptizer." That is quite a compliment, especially from Jesus.

Today's readings juxtapose the prophecy of Isaiah with the character of John. His voice was the threshing sledge, sharp and double-edged, that called people out of their religious doldrums into a new relationship with God. Parched souls were like the parched tongues of Isaiah's poem, people seeking refreshment from God. Of all places, they found their refreshment in the wilderness, with John, who turned their dried-up souls into springs of religious fervor. Like the prophets of old, John simply told the truth. God is always near. Always ready to forgive. Always instructing us and prodding us into the future. And like the prophets of old, John paid the price for such truth.

John the Baptizer is a hinge between all that prepared for Jesus and all that Jesus would do. His pivotal role in religious history is recognized by Jesus in this reading. Before we heap too much praise on John, before we allow ourselves just to look backwards, we need to remember another line of the gospel: "The least born into the kingdom of God is greater than John."

Jesus praises us, "the latter-day saints" who are reborn in our baptismal bath. All that John did was noble and necessary and part of salvation. But we, too, have a role to play as believers, as truth-speakers, as witnesses to Jesus. Advent is the celebration of God's presence through us and with us and in us. Even John the Baptizer could not ask for more.

Prayer

Lord God, what a life John the Baptizer led! He told your truth and lost his life. He knew that he was runner-up to Jesus, even though we call him "forerunner." How difficult it must have been to be so popular and so influential and to know that it was all for someone else. John served you well. Help me to seek more to serve than to be served, to find my own role, and to accept it joyfully and energetically. Let your presence shine through me in the way you choose. Amen.

Friday of the Second Week

Isaiah 48:17–19 • Psalm 1 • Matthew 11:16–19

"You can't please all the people all the time." That could be a sub-heading for today's gospel. A frustrated Jesus looks at the crowds and expresses his exasperation with their fickleness. There is always an excuse for not doing something we should, isn't there? Jesus, God-made-flesh, understands well that trait of our human nature.

When John the Baptizer was preaching, crowds trekked out into the desert to see this phenomenon, to hear his words. Some listened and changed. Most walked away. He was strange, after all. He promoted a rigorous diet of locusts and wild honey. He preached simplicity. He proclaimed the Word of God. His severity, like that of his prototype Elijah, was legendary. He just asked too much, it seems, and we see the response of the crowd: "He is mad!" With that dismissal, they felt free to return to their old ways.

Then Jesus came into their lives. His message was much the same: "Change your lives and believe in the gospel!" His way of preaching this message was completely different from John. Jesus did not withdraw into deserted areas but walked from village to village and taught in the synagogues. He went to parties, like the wedding feast at Cana. He frequented meals and banquets with the most unusual guest lists! Jesus ate and drank and enjoyed human company. The crowd, looking for an excuse, said that "this one is a glutton and drunkard." There was no way to satisfy the people who did not want to admit God into their lives.

Isaiah understood this, too. In the first reading today he reminds us that God, the Holy One of Israel, is the first and foremost teacher of the people. "I, the Lord your God, teach you what is for your good and lead you on the way you should go." That way is the path back to God. Even in Isaiah's time there were backsliders, people who just did not want to go to God.

Everyone has an excuse: "It's not what he did, but the way he did it." "I don't have time." "I'm too busy." "He is too severe." "He is too lax." "He is too liberal." "He is too conservative." And so on and so on. We all develop our excuses for not making this Advent work for us. There is a difference, however. We have heard these words and we have let them into our conscience, into our soul. If we are wise, we will heed the warning Jesus issues and acknowledge with Jesus that "time will prove where wisdom lies."

We are about halfway through Advent. Let us use our time wisely.

Prayer

Lord God, so many different personalities in these readings! Isaiah, John the Baptizer, Jesus. There should be something for everyone, but instead those who heard all looked for a reason to close their ears and their souls, and to continue in their old ways. What are my excuses? Help me to know them. What are my excuses? Help me to be more honest about them. What are my excuses? Give me the wisdom to stop making them and to use this Advent wisely. Amen.

Saturday of the Second Week

Sirach 48:1–4, 9–11 • Psalm 80 • Matthew 17:10–13

For the third day in a row the readings focus our attention on John the Baptizer, that desert-dwelling, word-spewing, truth-telling man of God. What a character he must have been to be remembered so constantly, so vividly by the audience of Jesus. How influential his example must have been for Jesus to use John continually as a point of reference.

People were fascinated by John. In today's world he would be a media hit, interviewed on all the right talk show programs, stirring up controversy in every corner. The evangelists portray him as a new Elijah, another man of powerful words and deeds who dared to speak the truth to kings and ordinary people alike. John was a man who challenged people to see the one-way path to disaster they were following by not putting God at the center of their lives. When God gets edged out, disaster follows. A society without God has no foundation. It has nothing to build upon but illusion and chimera.

The prophets were realists. They knew the human soul and they constantly called it back to God whose life it shares. So powerful was Elijah's influence in the life of ancient Israel that all kinds of legends developed around him. For example, when Jewish suffering became too great, legend had it that Elijah would intercede with God to move the clock of history ahead in order to shorten the period of suffering.

In today's gospel we see the popular belief that Elijah, who disappeared from this world in a whirlwind of fire, will return to the earth to prepare it for God before the end of history. Sirach, the wise teacher of today's first reading, describes Elijah's words as a burning furnace. Prophetic words had to be hot in order to penetrate the stone-cold souls of people who chased after other messiahs. There was always a singular purpose to such preaching: to bring people back to God. To change our hearts, our habits, our attitudes, ourselves.

Jesus speaks the same words in the gospel. His first public speech was a prophetic summons to prepare for the future by returning to God, by turning around from the path that was leading to disaster. In the gospel Jesus shows his familiarity with the prophetic tradition. He knows that he will pay the same price for truth as Elijah and John the Baptizer. He will be hounded and insulted, despised and ultimately put to death.

Elijah and John the Baptizer prepared the way for God's truth in our lives. They gave their all so that the living Word of God might find a people disposed to listen to truth. We are not required to do such dramatic things in our lives, but we are required to use Advent to listen. We need to listen to the prophetic word that disturbs us, that rouses us from our own spiritual coldness, and let the growing light of Advent penetrate our souls.

Prayer

Lord God, listening is so important. You send prophets and teachers to keep reminding us to pay attention to your words. Only your words can really help us, really change us, really make a difference in us. Many voices compete for our attention and claim to tell the truth. Help me at this halfway point of Advent to listen to you in your sacred Word, in the ways you speak to me in my daily life, in the voices of those who tell me the hard truths of the faith. Give me this Advent gift, the gift of a soul open to your Word. Amen.

THE THIRD WEEK OF ADVENT

"Rejoice Sunday." That is the subtitle for this Third Sunday in Advent. Years ago the violet or purple color of the vestments was altered for one day. The priest wore a rose-colored vestment to remind us that no matter how serious we are during this holy season, we also need to lighten up a bit, if not a lot, because Jesus is always with us.

Rejoicing is not something we do very often. In fact, seldom do any of us really "let go" and celebrate. Children do this the best. Adults tend to be more staid, more subdued. The dictionary offers some rather startling definitions for the word "rejoice": clap, shout, exult, festivity. On and on rolls the list of activities that describe rejoicing.

For most people, this season brings a great deal of hectic activity. Although much of it is oriented toward the celebration of Christmas, we tend to forget that the rejoicing is supposed to flow from a singular reason: the Lord Jesus. "Rejoice in the Lord always!" That is the advice of Saint Paul.

As the season of Advent moves closer to Christmas, perhaps we need to remember these words and be less frantic about all the other preparations. Some advice on how to observe this week of rejoicing might include:

1. Begin wrapping gifts today. Let the colored paper and ribbons bring you delight.

2. As you wrap each gift, offer a little prayer for the recipient, a reminder to yourself about why this person is special to you.

3. Light the third candle of your Advent wreath.

4. Attend a Christmas concert or play this week.

Third Sunday

Year A

Isaiah 35:1–6, 10 • James 5:7–10 • Matthew 11:2–11

"Be strong! Fear not! Here is your God! He comes to save you!" What headlines these words make. Each imperative from our Advent prophet Isaiah is a summons to faith. He offers these words in the midst of weakness. You see, the prophet always knows our human weakness. The prophet also knows God's power. That is the reason that the prophet can promise sight to the blind, hearing to the deaf, and dancing to the crippled. Only God has power to do this.

For us, it is early winter. In these parts, early December snowfalls have reminded us of what is to come. In our corner of God's vineyard the moisture of winter sends living things into hibernation, into rest. Summer's green is hidden from us and replaced by winter's gray. Just the opposite is happening in the Holy Land at this time. The rains are just beginning to fall, bringing life to the soil that the summer's dry heat has turned to dust.

Wherever that grace of rain falls, flowers and shrubbery suddenly blossom. The wilderness, to which our gospel continually leads us, becomes a garden. Dusty hillsides are transformed overnight into new growth for the sheep and goats.

The blooming promised by Isaiah fulfills itself before our eyes. Only God can do this. Only God can reverse the situation that people continually foul up. Only a God who wants to help—indeed to save—would act this way. Such is our God. That is the Advent message of Isaiah. Isaiah insists that this God of ours does not want to judge and destroy, but to bring life to us.

Advent also brings us back to John the Baptizer. His message from last week should still be ringing in our ears.

Reform! Revise! Repent! His toughness was legendary. His way was stern, promising God's fire of wrath on those who did not listen. Perhaps John never read this gentle, hope-filled passage from Isaiah. For the Baptizer, God's messiah was to be a figure of power, sweeping the land clear of evil-doers and invoking God's judgment on the wicked.

In today's gospel John the Baptizer sends his own disciples to investigate Jesus. Jesus' ministry of healing and good news has confused John. "Are you he who is to come? Or shall we look for another?" Gradually John came to understand: Jesus neither condemns nor punishes. There is only good news: God will act with power, but not the kind of power John foresees. God's power is found in surprising ways and unusual persons, like a messiah who is a servant.

We are now at the midpoint of Advent. At least chronologically, that's where we are. Where are we spiritually? What changes have we made? What preparations have we made? What kind of gift are we becoming for God and for others?

The blind, the mute, the deaf, and the lame of this gospel represent all the parts of our human lives that still need saving, that still need a messiah, that still need Jesus. Jesus cures them all, doesn't he? Advent calls us to prepare a way in our lives in which Jesus will be allowed more time and more space to weave his love and salvation into the fabric of our daily lives.

The great John the Baptizer wasn't initially convinced that Jesus was the one to come. A lot of the time our lives are like that—we look to something else to help us, to save us. Despite John's shortcomings, Jesus calls him the "greatest man born of woman." As wonderful as that title is, Jesus says we are even more fortunate. "The least born into the kingdom of God is greater than he." My friends, that's us, isn't it? No wonder our church calls this "Rejoice Sunday"!

John the Baptizer was a source of hope at the beginning of the gospel. Jesus is the fulfillment of that hope. We rejoice because this same Jesus brings us the power of God that can redirect our lives, that can save us. Listen again to the words of Isaiah, fulfilled in Jesus, given to us: "Be strong! Fear not! Here is your God! He comes to save you!" With the whole church we offer our Advent prayer: Come, Lord Jesus, do not delay!

Questions for Reflection

1. What things are you afraid of? Why? How can God come to help you this year?

2. Have you done anything about last week's resolutions to change?

3. What "delays" have you invented as excuses not to observe Advent properly?

4. Jesus says that every one of us is greater than John the Baptizer because we are born into the kingdom of God. How can you show that sense of dignity and joy in your life?

Third Sunday
Year B

Isaiah 61:1–2, 10–11 • 1 Thessalonians 5:16–24
John 1:6–8, 19–28

It is dawn. The rising sun is teasing colors out of the sky. Over the pond streaks of violet and pink reflect the solemn colors of our liturgical season. God's choice of hue this morning mocks those whose impatient faith has already decked their world in holiday red and green. For us who take the liturgical seasons seriously, it is still Advent.

The football games that seize our Sunday attention feature a half-time break, offering us a chance to catch our breath, to fix a snack, or to write a few more cards. No such luxury is given to us by Advent. At this halfway point in Advent the pace quickens. Our reflection deepens. Our seriousness about the coming of the Lord increases.

Ah, Advent. You summon us away from premature Christmas cheer. You call us back to the desert of John, to the desert of Jesus, and to the desert of our own souls.

Desert stillness contrasts with shopping mall chaos. Desert solitude seeks our souls. In the desert the barely discernable wind is but a quiet whisper, the Spirit starting anew in us. Renewal. Repentance. Change.

Today the hushed desert breeze carries a new sound. A message. Hope. In the deserted places along the serpentine shores of the Jordan River, a stranger appears and delivers a startling message. To those who have followed the twisting valley to this place of solitude, he says: "Make straight the way of the Lord!" Such a blessing—a straight path instead of the present contorted one!

A way for God. A highway for a new Exodus, an exodus from selfishness and sin, away from sickness and anxiety and death, a direct route into God's promise.

How odd that such a message of hope should encounter opposition. Some do not rejoice in these words, however. Like Scrooge, they scoff at the depths of human love, at the possibilities of peace, and at the prospect of a new future with God and with each other.

These doubters, priests and levites, are not skilled in the subtle craft of espionage. They speak directly to John and ask "Who are you? Elijah? the prophet? the messiah?" John is none of these. His answer is as simple as it is bold, as frank as it is humble, and as puzzling as his sudden appearance in the wilderness. "I am a voice," is all he says. "I am a voice in the wilderness." A voice of hope. A voice of truth. A voice raised up by God against injustice. A voice that will call cousin Jesus to the water. A voice that calls us to the water, to refresh our own baptism.

Advent beckons us to be voices, voices that speak out for the poor, that speak out against injustice. We are to be voices that raise words of praise and thanksgiving and rejoicing to God for his marvelous, mysterious activity in our world and within us.

What kind of word are we preparing to speak this Christmas? What word are we preparing to be as the Word becomes flesh in us this Christmas?

Questions for Reflection

1. When asked who he was, John said, "I am a voice." How would you answer?

2. What still needs to be done before Christmas? Is it worth worrying about, or should other things come first?

3. What ways has God been active in your life this Advent that are a direct result of the way you have chosen to observe the season?

4. What messy, crooked part of life does God still need to straighten out for you?

Third Sunday
Year C

Zephaniah 3:14–18 • Philippians 4:4–7 • Luke 3:10–18

It is still Advent. Advent—that strange time of the year when the world around us quickens its pace, and shouts that the time to buy things is here again.

It is also that season when our church tells us to slow down the pace, to tune out the noise, to wander around in darkness, to rummage around in the depths of our ordinary selves, and to make our souls silent and open to receive the gift of God's Son in new ways.

Here we are: trapped—as always—between the all too real world in which we live and work and the world of the kingdom of God for which we long. Two worlds. One of us. What should we do?

The Advent gospels always begin with the sobering message of the last judgment. Then the gospel quickly moves on to the preaching of John the Baptizer. His words are both unwanted yet true. Unwanted because no one ever wants a prophet around to bother us into behaving; true, because we know his words cut deeply into our souls. The time has come! This conscience-stabbing prophet embarrasses us with his holy call to worry more about God and less about other things. He reminds us of the two worlds in which we struggle.

The Word of God says, "Rejoice! Again I say rejoice!" But the world says, "Unemployment. Inflation. Winter heating bills. The kids need new shoes but want Nintendo games."

The Word of God says, "The peace of God which surpasses all understanding will fill your hearts and minds in Christ Jesus." The world says, "Spend more money for defense." The Word of God says, "Rejoice! The Lord is near!" But the world says, "Bah! Humbug!"

What do we do when confronted with such choices? All of us look for answers. Some modern messiahs say "Take this pill. Drink this beverage. Smoke this thing. Buy that thing." What kind of salvation is that?

John looks into our hearts. He makes us look at ourselves and offers practical answers to our questions. To the soldiers, John advises, "Don't bully people." To the tax collectors, John encourages, "Don't cheat."

If you are a mother or father, John would advise, "Be a good one. Make that your gift to your children, the gift of time and being there for them." To a student, John might say, "Study, and don't worry about grades. Just learn something, for God's sake." To a Christian, he would say, "So, what do you think about Advent? Do you pray? How are you preparing for the Lord? Dismiss all anxiety from your mind! Rejoice!"

Advent is a season when purple sobriety and tinseled festivity compete for our allegiance. It requires a choice between John the Baptizer and our favorite TV program.

Is our religion something we haul out of the closet and display once a year? Or is our God always present, comforting us, challenging us, loving us, coming to us in very human ways? With that ancient crowd we ask John, "What should we do?" I think we know the answer.

Questions for Reflection

1. Why do we so often feel trapped between the world of our religion and the world of our daily lives? Which one has the greater influence over you? Why?

2. "Have no anxiety." That's what God's Word says. What are you anxious or worried about, and how does it reveal what is really important to you?

3. What practical advice would John the Baptizer offer to you if he appeared at the door?

Monday of the Third Week

(Note: If today is December 17th or any date closer to Christmas, see pages 71-86 for the appropriate daily reflection.)

Numbers 24:2–7, 15–17 • Psalm 25 • Matthew 21:23–27

The bible has a sense of humor. That is clear from today's readings. Often we think of the bible only in the most serious terms, but when confronted with today's passages we see clearly that much can be learned from that side of life that catches us off guard. Perhaps it is quite appropriate that these first readings after "Rejoice" Sunday are intended to teach us through humor.

Our reflection begins with the episode of Balaam found in the Hebrew Scriptures. Balaam is a prophet. Hired by the King of Moab, he was supposed to deliver an oracle that was favorable to the Moabites but that would be a curse to the Hebrews. The Hebrews, you see, want to cross Moabite land on their way from Egypt to the Promised Land.

Often in the Hebrew Scriptures there are complaints against the false prophets, people who are paid to deliver a message favorable to leaders, favorable to the status quo. Balaam was such an instrument of royal will. But when he opened his mouth to curse the Hebrews, only words of blessing came out. Imagine his surprise! Imagine the anger of the king! He even tried a second time to earn his money, but only truth would issue forth from his lips. God's truth. The Hebrew people were destined for greatness because God's favor rested upon them.

The gospel continues the lesson. The leaders of the people, those who should know better, do not recognize Jesus for who he is—the chosen one of God. Instead of faith, they are filled with trickery, deceit, and envy. Their question is meant to embarrass Jesus. But Jesus won't be intimidated so easily. He uses their own ploy against them: a question for a question, a puzzle for a puzzle.

The leaders consult again, trying to resolve the dilemma. There is no way out of the position into which Jesus has forced them. They have no commitment: not to truth, not to God. They feebly answer, "We don't know." As a result, Jesus refuses to answer their question. In the process, however, he wins the duel of wits.

Jesus knows us well. Despite the deceit, trickery, envy, and lack of faith that so easily characterize our own response to Jesus, Jesus loves us. This is the human condition which he has chosen to share. This is the human condition that Jesus comes to reconcile to God.

There are many things we don't know about Jesus or our neighbor or ourselves. Too often our own response echoes the words of the hypocritical leaders who tried to trick Jesus. This we do know, however: Jesus is coming to us this year in new and surprising ways. Like Balaam, who was surprised at the words that issued from his mouth, we, too, get surprised by the things we do and the things we say. One of the joys of our faith is that God is always surprising us: with blessing, with forgiveness, with love, with Jesus.

Prayer
Lord God, help me to see your sense of humor, the way you tease me into finding you in new ways in my life. Help me to understand the way that reversals and disappointments and even puzzling events can bring me closer to you. I do believe, Lord, but my faith needs the support that comes from trying to live with your will for me. Help me to stop trying to figure it out and just to accept it. Amen.

Tuesday of the Third Week

(Note: If today is December 17th or any date closer to Christmas, see pages 71-86 for the appropriate daily reflection.)

Zephaniah 3:1–2, 9–13 • Psalm 34 • Matthew 21:28–32

Jerusalem. The very word evokes images of religion, of holiness. Jerusalem is the most honored of all cities.

Not so, says today's prophet in the first reading. Zephaniah disagrees with our romantic images of Jerusalem. He is a prophet, you see. A man who sees things as God sees them. Someone who speaks God's truth. He has very little regard for Jerusalem at the beginning of this passage.

Zephaniah bases his opinion on the moral fibre of the city rather than on its physical structures. The pilgrim may revere its ramparts, its walls, its history. But this chosen city of God, this heart of Israel's religion, this home of the temple, says today's prophet, is filled with filth and shame.

Zephaniah is a good prophet, true to his vocation. He doesn't simply describe the problem, he also offers its solution. Jerusalem's shame will be changed. Isn't that what prophets always call us to do—to change? Isn't that God's grace to us? We are allowed time to change. Thank God!

In Advent we are given four weeks of precious time to hear the gospel in new ways, to see our neighbor with kinder eyes, to look at our own mirror-images, and to alter what is not attractive. What we are summoned to change is not just our exterior. Face-lifting is not the object of Advent. Soul-lifting is. Advent summons us to lift our minds and hearts and souls to God. God changes Jerusalem's shame to holiness and peace. "I will change and purify the lips of my people." That's what God does.

Yesterday's readings had us ponder the words of the prophet Balaam. His lips were changed by God. Curse became blessing. Today we read about more words that change on our lips. This gospel is a perfect example.

The older son in oriental society has a great deal of privilege. He is the heir. He knows favor and preference his entire life. Externally this elder son plays his role to perfection. His response is immediate and obedient, the proper answer to his father's order. But inside this boy is filled with contempt for his father. He has no intention of following through on his words. He is like the Jerusalem of shame and filth that Zephaniah holds up in front of our eyes.

Younger sons seldom know the kinder side of their father's dispositions. This younger son is full of bluster and rebellion on the outside. Inside, he is respectful and obedient, the opposite of his older sibling. Yet he is the one who does his father's will and will be rewarded.

Jesus uses the parable to explain his ministry to the people whose outsides are rough and unacceptable. Prostitutes and tax collectors, the most despised trades of men and women, these are the followers of Jesus. The external nature of their work and the internal reality of their souls are no secrets to Jesus. Neither are we.

It is not easy to keep body and soul together, to unify our external and internal selves. When we do accomplish it, we have a sense of integrity and we become great gifts to God, to others, and to ourselves.

Prayer

Lord God, how often I am like the Jerusalem of Zephaniah, attractive on the outside but filled with problems on the inside. You know this and you love me anyway. You also know that I can do better, so you give me Advent, a time to be honest with myself and to change myself more and more into your own image and likeness. Help me to make myself a gift of beauty and faith on the inside wrapped in the packing of care for others and joy in your love. Amen.

Wednesday of the Third Week

(Note: If today is December 17th or any date closer to Christmas, see pages 71-86 for the appropriate daily reflection.)

Isaiah 45:6–8, 18, 21–25 • Psalm 85 • Luke 7:18–23

"Let justice descend, O heavens, like dew from above, like gentle rain let the skies drop it down." It is December, the month of clouds and darkness and long, lingering rain. It is a different rain than summer's violent storms. It falls steadily, sometimes melting away a recent snow. It seeps deep into the earth, where the life-giving moisture is stored for spring's new life.

The prophet known only as "Second Isaiah" wrote the words of our first reading and the words of the first sentence of this reflection. He focuses on the power of God to control creation, a creation that so often seems to be beyond us and out of control, especially out of *our* control.

The prophet is clear. It is the God of Israel who creates, who sustains, and who cares for creation. Without a doubt, God is in charge.

In this gospel we meet Jesus who is also in charge. He is in charge of fulfilling the words that Second Isaiah and the other prophets could only speak about, dream about, but never see. He bestows sight on the blind, hearing to the deaf, mobility to cripples, life to the dead. Only someone in charge of creation can do such marvels. Jesus shares God's creative, sustaining, caring power. This is the work he does. We call it ministry.

Jesus is also busy about the business of justice, of making things right, for God's sake. His answer to John the Baptizer's question is direct and truthful: Without doubt, he is "he who is to come." We need look for no other. We need wait no longer.

Not everyone wants justice, however. That is a sad truth

in our world. Some want all the comforts of life for their own use, and so they plot and plan against the Lord and his anointed, Jesus. To the greedy and ambitious, Jesus is a stumbling block in their effort to fulfill their heart's desires. To the faithful, Jesus is no stumbling block. He is, instead, a cornerstone, a foundation upon which all life rests.

Cornerstone or stumbling block? Justice for all or everything for a few? Our Advent meditation summons us to see the power of God at work in Jesus and in the church as a power for good, a power on our side, a foundation for our Christmas hope.

Prayer

Lord God, you are the master of the universe. You make all things and you guide all of history. You sent your prophets to keep this world on the right course. You sent John the Baptizer to call us back to yourself. Finally you sent your own Son, Jesus, as the Way. Jesus is the foundation of our lives, of my life. In the "busyness" of these days, help me to see the power of Jesus at work, healing our broken world, healing my own soul, bringing hope and joy to me through other people, and through me to others. Amen.

Thursday of the Third Week

(Note: If today is December 17th or any date closer to Christmas, see pages 71-86 for the appropriate daily reflection.)

Isaiah 54:1–10 • Psalm 30 • Luke 7:24–30

"'My love shall never leave you nor my covenant of peace be shaken,' says the Lord, 'who has mercy on you.'"

Such words of encouragement! So often we think of the prophets only in terms of doom and gloom, of negative messages filled with fire and brimstone. Not so in this prophecy. Again we are reading from the poetry and faith of the anonymous prophet we call "Second Isaiah." His message is uplifting and positive, encouraging and energizing. They are words much needed in a world that tends to wander far from God and God's Word. We need words like this, not just because they make us feel good, but because they are true. God's love for us overpowers any disappointment God might have with us. That is part of the gospel.

The words of today's gospel paint a different portrait. Once again the spotlight shines on John the Baptizer, that strange, strong character of faith. Our image of him is familiar: strange place, strange clothing, stranger diet. This is the formula that creates the strength and vigor of God's messenger to us in Advent.

Jesus has only positive words for this unusual man. The gospel continues yesterday's episode in which John sent emissaries to ask Jesus whether or not he was indeed the messiah. As they depart, Jesus shares his admiration for John with his own followers. John doubted, but he is not scolded for that doubt. In fact, he is commended by Jesus for seeking truth. Truth, after all, is the prophet's tool of trade. Words of truth that summon people to repentance can cut into our souls and expose us for who we really are.

The Pharisees and lawyers of this gospel did not appreciate such words. They heard no truth from John or from Jesus. They rejected the need to examine their lives and change. They thought they knew God. The sad truth is that they had closed their souls to God's word.

This gospel has a strange ending, one of the most unusual in the bible. We normally think that God always wins in the end, that God gets his way. But look! "The Pharisees and the lawyers, on the other hand, by failing to receive his baptism defeated God's plan in their regard." God wanted to help them, but it is possible to frustrate God's plan. What a haunting thought—that our own decisions, that our own way of listening and responding to God can likewise either advance or frustrate God's plan for us!

It is very close to Christmas, isn't it? How attentive have we been to John the Baptizer's call to rethink and reform our lives? How attentive have we been to our own baptism? How do we show our gratitude to God for the loving plan that redeems us?

Prayer
Lord God, for many days now we have been listening to your prophets as they call us to see ourselves with different, more honest, eyes. John the Baptizer saw the need for that kind of truth in our world and in each of us. Sometimes such truth can frighten us, but it doesn't have to. Help me to seek the truth about myself, and then to change as I must. Help me to see the way your truth can never hurt me because you always love me. Let the decisions of my mind and the thoughts of my heart lead me closer to you and to others as I make my way to Christmas this year. Amen.

Friday of the Third Week

(Note: If today is December 17th or any date closer to Christmas, see pages 71-86 for the appropriate daily reflection.)

Isaiah 56:1-3, 6-8 • Psalm 67 • John 5:33-36

In our "melting pot" society it is difficult to understand the way that ancient people felt about foreigners. In our country, everyone speaks the same language. One can travel a thousand miles in any direction and the language, culture, sights, and sounds remain quite similar.

It is not so in most of the world. A journey of a couple hundred miles or less brings you into another country with its own language and, often enough, another way of life. Foreigners in the ancient world were looked upon as exotic and were often viewed with fear or suspicion.

Isaiah's message today is that these foreigners are more faithful to the God of Israel than the people of Israel! Such an announcement did not earn him much favor, but prophets are used to that. Our prophet is actually the "Second Isaiah," a prophet who followed the general teachings of Isaiah of Jerusalem, but who applied them to new times and a new situation—life in a foreign land during Israel's Exile.

As a prophet, he saw reality in a different light than his co-religionists. He saw things as God did, thus his announcement that foreigners can be more faithful than Israelites.

In our Christmas season the same lesson is taught by the visit of the astrologers that is recorded in Matthew's gospel. They are non-Jews, outsiders. Yet they recognize Jesus for who he is, a king. They told a truth that Herod and his court could not accept. They gave witness to that truth by their presence and their presents at the manger.

Matthew's gospel tells us that a star led the magi to

Jesus. Since they were astrologers, this makes sense. We could say that "they saw the light." John's gospel, which we read today, speaks a lot about light. And witnessing. And truth.

The early church was often confused about the exact role of John the Baptizer and his relationship to Jesus. They were at pains to make it clear that, as important as John was, he was not the expected messiah. Jesus was. In this passage many wonderful qualities are used to describe John the Baptizer. But no one less than Jesus spells out the difference between the cousins. Jesus tells us that John was a "lamp." Jesus, however, is the light itself.

We can learn about God from many sources, often from surprising ones, like co-workers or neighbors we didn't quite trust, but who manage to show us their own light under surprising circumstances. Truth, witness to Jesus, and light. In our Advent quiet and reflection we are asked today to find Jesus, not always in the regular, expected places, but in the faces and experience and love of strangers, all of whom give hidden witness to Jesus.

Prayer

Lord God, most of us are shy people, tending to evaporate in a crowd. We worry about how others will receive us, what they will think of us. Your own Son came into our world, very much a stranger. Only a few welcomed him. Only a few were hospitable. In a world where people are pressured by their peers to be alike, to do the same things, to do the acceptable thing, help me not to be afraid to do what is right, to embrace my religion, to accept Jesus. Let me see the light leading me out of the darkness of my shyness and sin and fear into the brilliant radiance of your Son, the light of the world. Amen.

THE FOURTH WEEK OF ADVENT

Advent is almost over now. This final week sometimes lasts only a few days rather than a full week. In any case, it is a time that finds us busy with preparation. As the frantic pace of the world around us increases, our faith bids us to do the opposite. Week four of Advent is a time to slow down, quiet down, and take time for God.

The readings for the Fourth Sunday of Advent always focus our attention on Mary, the Mother of Jesus. The gospel asks us to ponder the mystery of the wonderful things that God does for us and in us and through us. Mary's response is perfect, an acceptance of God's will. The first thing she did afterward, however, was seek advice from another person, her cousin Elizabeth, who was also experiencing the unbelievable power of God in her life.

As this year's Advent slowly closes, be sure to take time to let these readings penetrate your soul, enliven your expectation of what God wants to do through you and for you. Then through the eyes of faith see the true marvel of Christmas: Jesus who came to Bethelehem long ago; Jesus who is always with us, even though sometimes hidden as though in a womb; Jesus who is coming at the end of time to transform our world into the world of the gospel he preached. Suggestions for the week:

1. Light the fourth candle on your Advent wreath while doing the readings of the day.

2. Prepare a small food parcel for a local food pantry.

3. Purchase and wrap a gift to give to the poor. Put a tag outside the wrapping indicating the age, sex, and size of the person for whom the gift is intended.

4. Listen to the words of your favorite Christmas carol. What new meaning do they have for you this year?

5. Visit someone who is shut in, calling first to see if there is anything they need.

Fourth Sunday
Year A

Isaiah 7:10–14 • Romans 1:1–7 • Matthew 1:18–24

It is still Advent. Not yet Christmas. Not in church anyway. Outside, the cold, crisp sparkling weather reminds us of the season. So does the darkness all around. Inside, cupboards are filling up with Christmas goodies. Greeting cards arrive from friends and relatives far and near. Treasures are lurking in closets. Decorations glitter everywhere—except in the churches, where it is still Advent. All these external things are signs of something. They are beautiful. But, Advent stubbornly reminds us, they don't really matter.

Today's prophetic reading tells us which signs truly matter: God's signs. God's words. Once again the Word of God bids us to part for a few moments from the commercialization of Jesus and turn our attention toward God's Jesus. If you've missed any of Advent, these readings quickly make up for it. They invite us to move deeply and quickly into the mystery of God.

"Behold, a virgin shall conceive and bear a son. She will name him Immanuel (God with us)." Such a sign! Such words are hard to understand. Like mystery, they are filled with promise. They are also filled with tension: the tension of a prophet scolding a powerful king, the tension of God's way confronting the world's way, the tension of faithlessness opposing faith, the tension of the present vis-à-vis the unknown future.

Advent is a good season for tension, isn't it? We've been experiencing it for some weeks now. Contrast the almost frenzied commercialization of the season (and our own participation in it) with the insistent message of Isaiah, John the Baptizer, and Matthew that there is something more, something deeper to which we ought to give our energies and attention. Our faith and our culture are at odds again.

The gospel is clear. Joseph and Mary knew about tension. Each of them wondered what in the world God was doing to them, through them. "How can this be?" asks a pregnant virgin. "How can this be?" asks a disappointed bridegroom. "What should I do?" each asks alone, in fear and in doubt. Aren't those the same questions we ask when God becomes involved in our lives in puzzling and mysterious ways?

Joseph's culture would have him send Mary away with a quiet divorce. The same culture would have Mary disappear in shame. But God's activity won out over the culture. Joseph took Mary as his wife. He trusted God's word. How easy could that have been? Mary did not flee. She, too, trusted God's word. She acted out of faith. Both trusted that despite all that was going on their lives, God was with them.

Each of us has tensions and problems and questions. This year, if Advent has taught us anything, it is that all the great biblical people shared this most human experience. We are in good company with Isaiah and John the Baptizer and Joseph and Mary. In the questioning and doubt and fear, they continued to believe. They believed in the power of a benevolent God to act on their behalf, despite the mysterious ways God chooses. They believed that God was with them, even in the most difficult moments of their lives. They believed. And so do we.

Surely in the last days of her pregnancy as in the first days described in this gospel, Mary took time to ponder the mystery of God's activity in her life. In this last week of holy Advent, take time to quiet your soul, to pray. See what Isaiah promised: God is with us. See what Joseph and Mary eventually saw: God coming to us. God giving himself to us. May these last hours of waiting be faith-filled, quiet, and holy.

Questions for Reflection

1. What tensions have been part of your Advent this year? How have they helped you to see the way God is trying to be present in your life?

2. Why do faith and culture often seem at odds with each other? Which element has more influence in your life?

3. What can you do in this last week of Advent to finish your spiritual preparation for Christmas?

Fourth Sunday
Year B

2 Samuel 7:1–5, 8–11, 16 • Romans 16:25–27
Luke 1:26–38

The time is the sixth month of Elizabeth's pregnancy. The story begins in Nazareth, an out-of-the-way village in central Galilee. The characters are: Elizabeth, an older woman who yearned all her life for a child; Mary, a young woman who was more surprised than Elizabeth to find out about her own pregnancy; an angel named Gabriel, "the Strong One of God," who brings the startling news to Mary and who also says, "Do not be afraid"; last, the Holy Spirit, whose presence and activity always catch us off guard, always surprise us. The occasion is the Annunciation, the solemn proclamation to Mary that God is doing something remarkable in her life.

In these weeks of preparation we have bumped into God in strange places. Today we are invited to tiny Nazareth, a backwater village if ever there was one. God, you see, always chooses the least likely people and places to work these marvelous deeds.

Elizabeth waited all her life for the child of promise she carries within. We have been waiting only four weeks. We have waited to see what marvels of wisdom and power God will bring into our lives this year.

In this gospel, Mary's time of waiting is just beginning. Our waiting, our yearly celebration of Advent, is almost finished. Once again we prepare to hear those words that echo in our Christmas souls: manger, swaddling clothes, shepherds, star, Three Kings, no room in the inn, Gloria in excelsis Deo, Bethlehem, Joseph, Mary, Jesus. For believers these are not ordinary words. They are faith-words, evoking images of the beginnings of Christian faith, the remarkable story of the birth of our remarkable Savior.

In these final, fleeting moments before Christmas, take time to ponder the mystery of it all—the depth of God's love and the hope generated in our world each year at this time because of this gospel, because of these words.

Before we get totally absorbed in the spirit of Christmas, the church gives us this gospel for one final moment of Advent pause. The spotlight focuses on Mary, the woman of faith who said "yes" to God when she first heard the gospel. She heard God's Word and accepted it. She let the Word become flesh in every possible human dimension. After the angel left her she had nine months to ponder what it all meant.

Now the time is our own day. The place is our own souls. The characters are you. And me. And the Holy Spirit. As Advent draws to a close, we take time to ponder what gifts God has given to us. Faith. Life. Each other. We reflect on our own "yes" to God. We take time to meditate on what sort of gift to God we have made of our own lives during this Advent season.

May our gift to God be an unqualified and faith-filled "yes" to God's Word becoming flesh within us. May the waiting have been happy and holy. May Christmas bring peace to Jerusalem. And to you.

Questions for Reflection

1. We are familiar with this gospel of the Annunciation. Less familiar to us are the thoughts that Mary would have had at such a moment. What made her able to respond to God's unbelievable initiatives with so much faith?

2. What are your earliest childhood memories of Christmas? How do they continue to be with you today as you make your own preparation for Christmas?

3. Mary said "yes" to God under difficult circumstances. To what is God asking you to say "yes" in your life?

Fourth Sunday
Year C

Micah 5:1–4 • Hebrews 10:5–10 • Luke 1:39–45

"My Soul in Stillness Waits." My parish has used this hymn at the beginning of each Advent liturgy this year. The organist begins the music softly, slowly. The ministers process into the church with only the sound of the music in the background. No words will be sung, not until everyone is in their place. Not until everything is ready. Then, slowly and deliberately the congregation joins in the quiet prayer of its church's Advent: My soul in stillness waits. Our souls in stillness wait.

It is an especially appropriate reflection for this fourth and final Sunday of Advent. We have been waiting for some time now for the end of this season filled with its solemn, brooding words. But instead of charging our energies to an uproar, the season has worked its wonder. If we have cooperated with it, we have slowed down. Quieted ourselves. We can wait in stillness for the marvel about to take place again: God's gracious gift coming to us again.

Today the church turns our attention away from the desert, away from John the Baptizer and the crowds of people strolling along the Jordan. Instead, we are transported to two insignificant villages. We are led by the Spirit to Bethlehem, the birthplace of David, Israel's greatest king, her strongest messiah. In her crooked streets merchants hawk their wares, children play their games, and all remember the glory that had once been hers. Jerusalem's glory long ago outshone that of Bethlehem.

The prophet Micah knows more about Bethlehem than most people. Prophets always do. He knows that this quiet, forgotten village will once again play a role in human history. With solemn cadence he announces that once again, out of this tiny place, a great thing will happen. Another, like David, will come forth from this place who will rule with justice and who will bring peace. But until his words come to pass, the souls of Bethlehem's inhabitants wait in stillness. In mystery.

The liturgy also bids us to travel to Ein Karem, a few hilly miles west of Jerusalem. There the priestly family of John the Baptizer dwelt in close proximity to the temple. There an impossible conception took place, and Elizabeth was with child. Her soul in stillness waited, too. Surely such a remarkable event must have been a portent of something special. Imagine the care she took during her pregnancy, this woman who waited all her life to be a mother. Imagine the stillness that surrounded her activity, all attention focused on her by family and neighbor—until Mary arrived.

Elizabeth was the first to recognize that something else remarkable and mysterious was taking place. God's power was alive in Mary. She was the first to greet the Lord who was waiting in the still silence of Mary's womb. Most people would be disappointed that the attention had shifted to another, but not Elizabeth. Her name means "God is fullness," for that is what God did for her. He filled her with new life. He filled Mary with new life. Their offspring would fill the world with new life from God.

Soon we will rejoice in Immanuel, God with us. With these readings we rejoice in the promise of his coming. We are still an Advent people. We wait in quiet darkness, like new life in the womb. Our souls in stillness wait. God's gift to us is like a wrapped package that lies shrouded in mystery under the Christmas tree. In many sizes and colors and shapes, God makes us wait to unwrap the mystery of this Christmas.

There is a wonderful Hebrew word for faith. It carries with it the notion of waiting. Isn't that what faith and life and hope are really about? We wait to see how it will all turn out, and in the meantime we trust in God.

The application is so simple, so human. Elizabeth and Mary no longer wait. We are the waiting ones. We watch in hope, like a pregnant woman. We await to see what will come to life in us and for us because of faith.

Like Micah and like Luke, we are filled with hope. Like Elizabeth we are filled with wonder. Like Mary, the promise takes flesh in our lives and is always waiting to be born. Meanwhile, until Christmas, our souls in stillness wait.

Questions for Reflection

1. God chose Bethlehem as the birthplace of Jesus. Now God chooses us as the agents who will bring the Son into the world. How do you see yourself cooperating with God in this great, often quiet, work of bringing Jesus into the world?

2. Waiting and faith go hand in hand. How well have you waited this Advent? How has the quiet waiting revealed God to you?

3. What part of your life still needs to quiet down and wait for the Lord?

THE FINAL ADVENT WEEKDAYS

Beginning with December 17th and continuing through December 24th, the church selects special readings for the daily Eucharistic celebrations during the eight-day period before the birth of the Savior.

Use the meditations given here for December 17-24 on the appropriate weekdays. On the Fourth Sunday of Advent, however, use the meditation for the Fourth Sunday rather than the reflection given for that particular date.

The readings for these final Advent weekdays intensify the themes of watching and waiting and hoping. There are also renewed pleas for stillness, and an increasing number of promises of peacefulness and joy in the kingdom of the Messiah.

The events leading up to the first Christmas, especially the activities of Mary and Joseph and Elizabeth and Zechariah, take center stage in the gospels for these days. In a special way they call us to reflect on the mysterious and powerful presence of God in our lives and in our world.

There is a special canticle for each of these final Advent weekdays. Because they all start with the phrase "Come, O . . ." they are referred to as the "O Antiphons." They are taken from Evening Prayer of the Liturgy of the Hours where they are used as the antiphon or refrain for the Magnificat, Mary's hymn of praise recorded in Luke 1:46–55.

The "O Antiphons" are printed at the start of each day's reflection. Try to commit this brief verse to memory and call it to mind throughout the day.

December 17

Genesis 49:2, 8–10 • Psalm 72 • Matthew 1:1–17

Come, O wisdom of our God most high, guiding creation with power and love. Teach us to walk in the paths of knowledge!

Ever since the book and television program *Roots*, Americans have shown a renewed interest in discovering their origins. Amateur genealogists search through countless city archives and church records looking for traces of information about their families. There is a certain curiosity about where we come from that helps us to understand, maybe even to accept, who we are.

There are also problems with the discoveries that are made. Not everyone's family tree reaches back into some long-forgotten royal family. In fact, most of us descend from rather ordinary folk. Some even discover that their ancestors left other lands because of embarrassing, better-forgotten, circumstances.

The gospel of Matthew begins with the family tree of Jesus. Some churches display a "Jesse tree" in this season, a reminder of the theological background of Jesus. Whenever genealogies appear in the bible, readers usually wince at the long and strange names they must read. It seems a bit like reading the telephone book: a lot of truth, but not much excitement.

Even in this gospel list of the origins of Jesus' father's family, most names on the list are relatively unknown. A few names stand out, but the rest are obscure at best.

The list is a "who's who" of the royal families of Judah that reflects a promise of power made by the patriarch Jacob on his Egyptian deathbed. Most of these names mean little to us today. To the ancient believer, however, the list was not only a who's who, but a truthful list that included many unsavory characters. They are listed "warts and all," in the same way we would include the horse thieves and illegitimate ancestors on our family tree.

Some of the characters are foreigners who didn't even believe in the one God of the Hebrews. Never mind that, though: The list is true. Others are evil, faithless kings, hardly the paradigm of leadership for God's people. Not many women are listed, but those who are had interesting stories to tell!

Matthew is honest about these family origins. Jesus was born into a real world, into a real family. He lists three sets of fourteen generations. To this day, in the Church of the Nativity in Bethlehem, a fourteen-pointed silver star marks the spot where tradition says Jesus was born. The points of the star represent these fourteen generations. The list of royal ancestors also shows that Jesus would later have the right to be hailed as the messiah. Every king of Israel was a messiah, an anointed one.

We all come from families. Each family is a wonderful assortment of characters, some holy, some rascals. The heritage of Jesus is much like our own: rich, interesting, of mixed goodness. This gospel genealogy teaches that Jesus, who is truly of divine origin, is also truly born into our human world. He is one of us.

Prayer

Lord God, you sent your only Son into our human world. What a comfort to know that Jesus was born into a family, just as we are. What a relief to know that the family background of Jesus wasn't perfect either. On this late day of Advent, help me to understand my own family better, to love them even more, even when there are problems. Today I pray for myself and my family. Bless us, Lord, with your love and a lot of human patience. Amen.

December 18

Jeremiah 23:5–8 • Psalm 72 • Matthew 1:18–24

Come, O leader of ancient Israel, giver of the law to Moses on Sinai. Rescue us with your mighty power!

Most United States citizens are impressed by the royalty of other nations. While these countries debate the value of having royal families, we are fascinated by the whole idea, even though the founding fathers of our country rejected royal rule in favor of our fledgling experiment in democracy.

In the first reading, we see that the prophet Jeremiah was not impressed by royalty. His people had been under the royal thumb for some five hundred years. Seldom in that long stretch of time had there been a king worthy to rule God's people. The early prophet Samuel had warned about this inevitable development, but people are stubborn, and the bible tells us that both God and the prophet gave in to their whims.

During much of Jeremiah's unhappy life, Zedekiah was the king of Judah, the southern kingdom. The name Zedekiah means "My justice is God." This is a noble name and a bold claim, but Zedekiah never lived up to its promise.

In this prophecy Jeremiah courageously announces that someday a better king will come along, a more worthy ruler for God's beloved people. This new messiah will do what other kings have failed to do. This king will have a name similar to the incumbent king but the name is just different enough that everyone catches on to Jeremiah's true meaning. This new king will be called "The Lord our justice." It is a bold statement for Jeremiah to make and he will pay dearly for his integrity. In the midst of the political pollution of his time, he proclaims that a better king is coming, one who will rule rightly.

Our gospel today is set among circumstances quite opposite from Jeremiah's situation. To be sure, evil leaders were lurking around, but the setting is not a royal palace or people clad in royal purple. Today's gospel focuses on the humble Mary and her husband Joseph. Unlike that ancient king who was sure he had all the answers to his difficulties, we have seen in the Advent gospels that Mary and Joseph were honest and humble before God. They were filled with questions about what was going on in their lives.

When the messenger of God tells them not to fear, they listen. Joseph, the humble workman, listens and obeys. Mary, the questioning virgin, listens and obeys. In the midst of their questions while the mystery of God was hovering all about them, they listened and accepted God's activities in their lives. Their response is the opposite of the royal family.

Perhaps that is the reason why this is the beginning of the gospel. The gospel, you see, always stands opposite the world in which it is proclaimed and lived. The gospel always announces the end of tired, old, sinful ways and the beginning of new ways of relating to God and each other. It is the beginning of salvation.

Jeremiah reversed the name of the fickle king. This child of promise will bear a name that brings hope—God is with us. Immanuel. This child of promise shares his destiny and his identity with us: Christian. Anointed One.

Prayer
Lord God, so often in the bible you tell us not to fear, that you are here, and that you are in control. Often our lives seem out of control, manipulated by others. That is when we fear. On this Advent day, help me to trust more in your power to help me. Open for me the way to see that you love me and that you are in control of my life. Let the coming of your Son give me this confidence. Amen.

December 19

Judges 13:2–7, 24–25 • Psalm 71 • Luke 1:5–25

Come, O flower of Jesse's stem, sign of God's love for all people. Save us without delay!

The town of Zorah has rested since ancient times about fifteen miles west of Jerusalem in the fertile valley known as the Shephelah. There we meet the main characters of today's first reading, a man named Manoah and his wife. They have no children, for the wife is barren. Our narrator never even tells us the woman's name! Her lot in history begins in barrenness and ends in obscurity. How often this occurs in the bible!

A man. A woman. No child. Then an angel appears, bringing the word of God that always changes our human fortunes. A promise is made. A son will be born, consecrated from the womb. No wine or strong drink. He will be filled with God's own spirit. He is Samson.

The gospel advances us almost a thousand years in time, but only a few miles in place, to Ein Karem, another small village west of Jerusalem. There we meet another man. Another woman. Like the unnamed mother of Samson, she too is barren. A man. A woman. No child. Then an angel. Gabriel. A promise is made. A son will be born, consecrated from the womb. No wine or strong drink. He will be filled with God's own spirit. He is John the Baptizer.

In the account from the Hebrew Scriptures, the angel appeared to the woman. In Luke's gospel, Gabriel appears to the father, the priest Zechariah. Samson is noted for his physical strength, derived from his fidelity to God. John the Baptizer is also remembered for his fidelity to God, and every description of his strange desert life would indicate that he, too, was physically strong.

The angel Gabriel was busy those days, first a visit to Zechariah, soon a visit to Mary. Both times this messenger of God speaks God's promise, reveals God's saving plan beginning to take root in people.

Zechariah doubted and was struck dumb. Mary would question all that was going on, but would accept the mystery taking place in her life. So many parallels between the two! So many differences!

Our late Advent stillness brings quiet time for us to hear God's Word, perhaps not through angelic intermediaries, but certainly in new and wonderful ways. God is still at work in our world, revealing, speaking. How will we listen these last days?

Prayer

Lord God, these days are filled with wonder and mystery. As we move closer and closer to Christmas, you ask us to believe more deeply in the mysterious ways that you act in our world and in our lives. Zechariah and Mary both heard your word. So often my own response is more like Zechariah. I doubt and get confused. Help me to be more like Mary, to ponder quietly and accept faithfully your will for my life. Amen.

December 20

Isaiah 7:10–14 • Psalm 24 • Luke 1:26–38

Come, O key of David, open the gates of God's eternal kingdom. Free the prisoners of darkness!

Hundreds of greeting cards are fluttering through the mail at this very moment. Many of them have these familiar words from the prophet Isaiah inscribed upon them: "Behold, a virgin shall be with child, and bear a son, and shall name him Immanuel." For many, it is probably the only words of the prophet they know by heart. They have become so familiar, however, that the real power behind them gets obscured in the romanticism of our Christian holiday.

The prophet Isaiah lived in difficult times. The king mentioned in this text, Ahaz, is one of the most faithless, most evil kings in Judah's history. An encounter between prophet and king in the bible is never a happy occurrence. Two worlds collide: that of God and that of politics. This meeting is no exception.

In the same passage we learn that the prophet, the man of God, is walking with his son. The king is returning from an area in which child sacrifice was illegally practiced. His own offspring were victims. Life and death meet each other on that unhappy path outside Jerusalem. That is the way it always is when God confronts our world with truth: God's life versus the foolishness of the world.

The false piety of the king spurs the prophet to speech and to action. His promise of a future good king is a bold statement to make to the reigning evil king. The point is clear: God intends better for his people. Some future messiah/king will outshine the pride of this rascal.

We know that Jesus is the Messiah. There is no surprise

for us in hearing this familiar gospel again. The early Christians were convinced that Jesus fulfilled the expectations of the faithful men and women of long ago, even though they would not have thought in terms of such a far distant future.

This gospel continues where yesterday's gospel ended. The angel Gabriel is working overtime bringing God's good and surprising news. Yesterday a barren woman is told she will bring forth new life, a life touched by God. Today, a virgin of Nazareth is told that she will bring forth new life, a life also touched by God. Two impossible pregnancies! Two women left wondering what was happening to them. These are indeed unusual signs from God, signs that only prophets and deeply faithful people can accept, much less comprehend.

Christmas is very near now. These well-known texts can easily pass us by. That would be a great pity because both prophet and evangelist are summoning us to take some final quiet Advent time to ponder the meaning of the words and their mystery as they enter our lives this year.

What signs of his presence is God giving us this year? What does it mean to say "Let it be done to me as you say"?

Prayer

"Let it be done to me as you say." O God, these words are so noble. We pray something like that each time we offer the Lord's Prayer, "Thy will be done." The truth, though, is that often I want my will to be done. On this Advent day, as the excitement of Christmas nears, help me to see how I do your will, how I cooperate in your plan, just like Mary. So often I focus on the negative aspects of my spiritual life. Help me today to see and to celebrate all the good things, all the faith that is your gift to me. Amen.

December 21

Song of Songs 2:8–14 or Zephaniah 3:14–18
Psalm 33 • Luke 1:39–45

Come, O radiant dawn, splendor of eternal light, sun of justice. Shine on those lost in the darkness of death!

The Song of Songs (Canticle of Canticles) is rarely used in the lectionary. In fact, we read from it only six times. This is due to the fact that this short book is composed of poetry that is difficult to understand and filled with images that are both ancient and erotic. The book is a beautiful paean about God's love for his people. So much of the bible tells the story of God's love that it should be no surprise that sooner or later a song would express that love.

Today's selection from the Song of Songs fits beautifully into our late Advent meditations. God is portrayed as a lover, anxious to arrive and to see his beloved. Isn't that what every Advent is all about? God coming to us, God more anxious to see us than we sometimes are to see God?

In case the imagery of the Song of Songs is too obscure or risque for some ears, the church offers another reflection for our consideration. The quotation from Zephaniah is likewise little known, but powerful. Here, too, God is described as the one who rejoices, who sings because finally God has the chance to be with us! We don't often think of ourselves as so desirable to God, but these two readings make it clear: God can't wait for us, so God hurries into our lives. Rejoicing and dancing God comes to visit.

The gospel takes us back to Ein Karem, the home village of Zechariah, Elizabeth, and John the Baptizer. Mary and Elizabeth are the central characters. Can you imagine the stories that they had to tell each other? Angels. Pregnancies. Mysterious comings and goings. God's mystery taking flesh in each of them.

They rejoiced to see each other. Perhaps they understood the mystery as no two other people could! In the Hebrew Scriptures God rejoiced and danced at the chance to visit his people. Here, in the gospel, John the Baptizer begins to dance in his mother's womb when God, mysterious and hidden in Mary's womb, comes to visit.

We tend to treat godly things with boring solemnity. Each reading today offers us the image of joyful abandon in the presence of God. All of this can take place because of God's promise, God's Word. Elizabeth greeted Mary with the prayerful statement, "Blessed is she who trusted that the Lord's words to her would be fulfilled."

It is nearly the end of Advent. Our own patient waiting is beginning to pay off. Trust can be hard. It had to be difficult for Elizabeth and Mary, but they trusted nonetheless. Elizabeth had prayed all her life for a child. God heard her prayers in ways she never expected. God is full of surprises. God hears our words and rejoices when we listen to the Word of God, trusting that the promises of faith will come to pass for us, giving God cause to rejoice.

Prayer
Lord God, how often I feel that I am distant from you, yet your word today tells me that you love me and want to be close to me. You even rejoice over me! Help me to understand the value that I have, that I am, because I am made in your image and likeness, just like your Son, Jesus, who becomes one of us at Christmas. Increase my sense of self-worth, Lord. Let me rejoice in knowing that you are always coming closer to me. Amen.

December 22

1 Samuel 1:24–28 • (Response) 1 Samuel 2 • Luke 1:46–56

Come, O king of all nations, source of your church's unity and faith. Save all humankind, your own creation!

One of the most unusual episodes of the Hebrew Scriptures begins our reflection today. Hannah had prayed and prayed for a child. At last she gave birth to a son and named him Samuel. But after just a few verses in which we read of her piety, we also read that she left her own flesh and blood at the shrine with the old priest Eli. The story of Samuel's origin was unusual, but this ending to the episode is extraordinary!

Samuel grew up to become one of early Israel's greatest leaders, a judge who brought God's wisdom to the tribes, and a prophet who brought God's word to everyone. His most powerful tool was speech, a word, the Word of God. This portion of the first book of Samuel does not give us these details about Samuel's life. We know them from later chapters. We are left at the end of today's reading in mystery, wondering how a mother could do such a thing, could give up her only son for so uncertain a future.

What is not written is that Hannah was a woman of faith. She let God use her flesh to bring wisdom and direction to a people in search of guidance.

The movement from today's first reading to the gospel is not a smooth one, at first sight anyway. The gospel is a continuation of Luke's incredible narrative about two women of faith, Mary and Elizabeth.

The text is the Magnificat, the great prayer of Mary which is heard on several feasts of Our Lady and which is prayed every night in the Evening Prayer (vespers) of the church.

Like Hannah, both Elizabeth and Mary bore sons. Like Hannah, both gave them over to God's service as powerful preachers of truth, powerful witnesses to God. Just as Samuel reversed the flow of history by directing the leadership of Israel, both John the Baptizer and Jesus initiated a series of reversals: from sin to holiness, from faithlessness to faith, from being lost to finding a way to God.

This wonderful song speaks about those reversals: the power of God to undo the direction of history, to change the human heart. Mary announces that the poor will be rich, the hungry will eat well, while the spoiled will starve. The proud will be scattered, like the Tower of Babel of old.

Mary's own faith is summarized in this song from the pen of Luke. God's ancient promises are kept.

Mary speaks these words while the Son of God is taking flesh within her, while the eternal Word of God is becoming flesh in her so that it becomes part of us.

The gospel ends with a startling parallel to the first reading. After a magnificent act of faith, Hannah returns home. After assisting Elizabeth, Mary does the same. In our late Advent meditations, no matter how wisely or foolishly we have used the time of Advent, we still have a chance to come home to God.

Prayer

Lord God, women of faith in the bible have such hard stories to tell! Despite tragedy and puzzlement, each of them does your will. Each of them helps in some way to advance your plan of salvation. Hannah, Elizabeth, and Mary were not too proud to let you use them. Use me, Lord. Let me be open to your will and to your plan. Make a deeper faith one of the gifts you give me this year. Amen.

December 23

Malachi 3:1–4, 23–24 • Psalm 25 • Luke 1:57–66

Come, O Emmanuel, God's presence among us, our king and our judge. Save us, Lord our God!

"Who can stand when he appears? Who can endure the day of his coming? He will purify them." These are strong words from a strong prophet. They are the words of a man convinced of his mission and his calling.

Listen to these words from the reading of the day: "I will send Elijah to you, to turn the hearts of the fathers to their children and the hearts of the children to their fathers."

That is what God's word has been doing throughout this season, reversing the situation in which we live and making it smooth again, making it right again, bringing God back into the world God created and in which we live.

The prophet Elijah is invoked, that fiery man of God who suddenly appeared in Israel of old and just as suddenly disappeared in a chariot of fire. Many legends developed about Elijah, including the one alluded to in Malachi—that before the world will end, God will send Elijah back to earth. To this day, at the Passover meal of the Jews, an extra cup of wine is set at the table, just in case this is the year in which Elijah will make that famous return.

Luke saw things differently. He saw Elijah's return in the figure of John the Baptizer.

In this gospel, more of John the Baptizer's origins are recounted, including the bestowal of his name: John, gift of God. That was John's vocation: to be God's speech to us, a gift that calls us back.

When John's birth was predicted, his father Zechariah did not believe. He did not listen to God. His disbelief brought about a punishment: He became mute. This priest of God, who should have known better, was a poor witness to God's power. Zechariah, however, learned from his error. After the miraculous birth of John to his barren wife Elizabeth, he followed the instruction of God's messenger and allowed the name John to be given to the infant. God returned his gift of speech, and fittingly enough, Zechariah's first use of this restored gift was to praise God.

We are called to do likewise. In the silence that was imposed upon Zechariah, he learned the need to praise God. In our own Christmas preparation, despite all the "busyness" that comes our way, we need to find the silence that will teach us how to praise God this year.

The gospel also says that the whole neighborhood was afraid because of what had happened at Zechariah and Elizabeth's house. "What will this child be?" That was their fear. The child was nothing less than God's chosen instrument. Many people still fear those voices of truth, those voices of faith that believing people raise in praise of God.

"Was not the hand of the Lord upon him?" That was their second question. The answer is YES. That same hand of the Lord rests upon us when we recognize the proper time for silence and the proper time for praise. The hand of God rests upon us, calling us to a few more hours of patient waiting and to a lifetime of joyful praise.

Prayer

Lord God, rest your hand upon me. Help me to be like Elijah whose name meant "Yahweh is my God." Help me to be like John, whose name meant "gift of God." Help me to be faithful to my name, Christian, which means "anointed." You are Immanuel, God with us. Make me confident that I, too, am part of your plan and that you are with me. For this great gift, I thank you and praise you. Amen.

December 24

2 Samuel 7:1–5, 8–11, 16 • Psalm 89 • Luke 1:67–79

Most of us live in comfortable homes. Whether they are large or small, urban or suburban, apartments or single-family homes, they are comfortable and they are ours. It is hard sometimes to imagine that our own twentieth-century homes, no matter where they are or what they are like, are more comfortable than the palace of David, king of Israel. Even though David's home is described in this first reading as made of cedar, even though he may have had servants to do his bidding, our own homes have more amenities than he could have imagined.

David is a multi-faceted individual. He is a man of war and a man of peace, rascal and sinner, yet pious and God-fearing. He sees that his own dwelling is luxurious while the dwelling of the ark of the covenant is only a tent. Pious David intends to build a dwelling for God, a temple worthy of God's glory, a temple which will also bring David fame and fortune.

But it was not to be. David's plan was not God's plan. Human plans seldom are. It would fall to David's son and successor, Solomon, to build the famous temple of Jerusalem. God's plan for David was to build a dynasty, not a house. Thus, on this day before Christmas, we hear the famous prophecy of Nathan, that a ruler from the house of David will guide the fortunes of God's people. This was the kind of dwelling God preferred: faithful people, not elaborate buildings.

Today's gospel, like yesterday's, is a song, a theological poem that expresses the fulfillment for which David longed. The promise made to David comes to pass because, unlike us, God is faithful to promises.

This gospel, the Benedictus, is prayed by the church every morning in the Liturgy of the Hours. As dawn greets the day, these words greet the faithful. They come from the lips of Zechariah, the father of John the Baptizer, the man whose lips had once been closed because of his lack of trust in God's word. Now these same lips offer profuse praise, reviewing all of God's promises to Israel's ancestors and predicting the fulfillment of those promises in John the Baptizer and Jesus.

All these blessings form a proper meditation for our final hours before Christmas. The faithful people of old, prays Zechariah, have been rewarded for their patient waiting. Now we who have waited throughout Advent gain our reward, too.

God's light shines on us who have waited in Advent's darkness. God's peace is the blessing for us who have let the prophets' words disturb our souls and redirect our lives.

The canticle begins with the ancient Hebrew prayer, "Blessed be the Lord, the God of Israel." Indeed, blessed be God who keeps his promises to us. Blessed be God who sends us Jesus. Blessed, too, are we who are ready to greet Jesus in the joyful dawn of the morrow, Christmas.

Prayer

Blessed are you, O Lord. Blessed beyond our imagining. We bless you because of all you do for us. We bless you for all the gifts you give to us. On this last day of Advent, as Christmas edges into our lives, we praise and bless you for this season of quiet and darkness, this season of wonder and challenge. Even if we have not kept a perfect Advent, you still come to us. For that, we thank you. You give us so much, yet we ask for more. Today we offer the one gift to you that is adequate: our praise and our thanks for your gift of life and your gift of love. Amen.

Christmas Day

Isaiah 9:1–6 • Titus 2:11–14 • Luke 2:1–14

Winter dawn comes early to Bethlehem. The Church of the Nativity is beginning to empty out as pilgrims walk in the early morning dawn from the site of the birth of Jesus to the shepherd's fields where the morning Mass will be celebrated. For some hours now all the world has focused its attention on this tiny village, on this ancient church, and on this most holy site: a cave and a manger. Hardly the place to look for God, is it?

God existed in eternity, long before Christmas. God saw everything, but now God would see this imperfect world of ours as we are. When the creator of the universe came to earth, he cried, as all newborn infants cry: a cry of outrage at the condition of our world, a cry of freedom at release from the womb. A human voice. That is what God wanted, so God came to Earth.

Like all infants, the baby closed his eyes when he cried, hoping to return to the safety of the womb's darkness, to the way things were before birth, before creation. It was not to be. In fact, nothing would ever be the same again because of this night.

The child saw all sorts of things. He saw a man, confused at the events changing his life, and a woman who was little more than a child herself.

What did this baby dream the first time he closed his eyes? What did he hear with his human ears? The bleating of sheep? The coarse talk of shepherds? An innkeeper demanding payment? Mother and father murmuring softly over their desperate situation? These are the sounds of humanity that God wanted to hear, and God heard them in Bethlehem that first Christmas night. Hardly what one expects God to hear or to see, is it?

This is the marvel of it all! God chooses to be like us and at the same time calls us to be like God, Holy. God chooses to know the pain of humanity: our suffering and our joy, our giving birth and our dying, our poverty and our riches, our beauty and our ugliness, our want and our plenty. All of it is present in this Christmas story, isn't it? The baby sees it all: eyes peering at him. The eyes of a shepherd who had forgotten God. The eyes of a curious soldier who would one day beat him. The eyes of parents, hovering, worrying, protecting, as parents always do. The whole world comes together at Christmas in order to see God. To see God. But instead humanity saw so much of itself.

It is now dawn in Bethlehem. The day's beginning is almost over. The ancient pattern of that city has changed little since that night. Bethlehem teaches the world a lesson: Bethlehem was full of danger that first Christmas night. There was a restlessness everywhere. There were signs everywhere. Shadows and stars, strangers and soldiers. Bethlehem, you see, is always in danger.

The danger is that we will focus all of our attention "over there" and "in those days." Bethlehem and Christmas, my friends, are not about a baby. That already happened. Bethlehem and Christmas are about today. Here. Right now. Look at your own hands. Look at the person sitting next to you. See the humanity. That is what Bethlehem and Christmas are about. In each of us God has chosen to use our human ears and our human eyes and our human hearts and our godly souls.

To look only backward and far away is not the lesson of Christmas. That is very safe. To do only that is to betray Christmas. Christmas exists to push us, not backward, but into the future, God's future.

Christmas means not buying gifts for your children, but being there for your children. Christmas means seeing in the unborn the promise of life. Christmas means seeing a new sense of direction in your life. Christmas means seeing in our own, frail human flesh what God saw: something worthy of attention, something worthy of love, something worthy of life, something worthy of eternal life.

Christmas exists to show us that our God, the creator of the universe, the all-powerful, all-present God works in the strangest places and in the strangest ways, and in the strangest people: in you and in me. What we sense around us this day and what we feel so good about these days is the absolute fact that we can understand something about this mystery of faith, this incarnation, this God becoming one of us. When we perceive the full ramification of our creedal words, "The Word became flesh and dwelt among us," then love is born. Then hope is born. Then peace is born. Then righteousness is born. Then joy is born. Then Jesus is born.

What we celebrate today is not just the fulfillment of ancient prophecies, but the reality of God's life and love and energy being reborn in our faith, and in our hope, and most of all, today, in our genuine love for one another. God bless you. All of you. All of us.

Prayer

Thank you, God, for your presence, for rewarding our Advent stillness with your dynamic gift of self, for sanctifying our human flesh by dwelling as one among us. Open our eyes to the wonder of your glory, your power, your light, your Christmas peace. Let us experience the gift of the kingdom that you brought to earth on that first Christmas day. Help us today to bring your love and your gifts of goodness and peace to all the people we meet and all the people we think about on this holy, but hectic, day. O Come, O Come, Immanuel.

Additional Advent Feasts

Just as the world does not stop during the Advent Season, so, too, the church continues to celebrate the heroic lives of its saints in the weeks prior to Christmas. It also remembers two significant events in the life and devotion of Our Lady during the days of Advent.

The Solemnity of the Immaculate Conception is celebrated on December 8th to commemorate Mary's sinless conception in the womb of her mother Ann. This miraculous event is solemnized exactly nine months before Mary's birth which the church celebrates each year on September 8th. While this solemnity is celebrated throughout the world, it has special significance in the United States. Our Lady of the Immaculate Conception is honored as the special patroness of the United States. The national shrine in Washington, DC, is named in her honor.

The Feast of Our Lady of Guadalupe (December 12) has special significance for the country of Mexico and all people of Mexican heritage. This feast celebrates Mary's appearance in 1531 to Juan Diego on a hillside outside Mexico City, and continues today to strengthen the faith of this nation and its people.

You may choose to meditate on the reflections for the feasts of Our Lady and the three saints listed here (Andrew, Nicholas, and Lucy) on the date of their feast or you may wish to use the reflection for the appropriate day of the Advent Season.

Saint Andrew
November 30

Romans 10:9–18 • Matthew 4:18–22

I have a good friend who is a dedicated, compassionate, energetic priest. Like most of us, he has wonderful qualities of faith and humor. Those often go together. One of his exaggerated fears is that he will become a martyr. He doesn't fear martyrdom as such. His real fear is that, should this happen, he will only be listed in the liturgy as one of the companions of some more famous person.

Today's feast reminds me of him. We celebrate an apostle and martyr, Andrew. He is the brother of Peter, the most favored apostle and the first pope. In the biblical lists of apostles Andrew is always mentioned as the brother of Peter, never the other way around.

Many people gain their fame by association with famous people. Some do it on purpose. It is a way to get noticed. For others, it is an accident of birth or timing. With Andrew, we never know. Who was the older brother? What was it like for Andrew to live in the shadow of Peter?

When significant moments occur in the life of Jesus, it is always Peter, James, and John who are favored to participate. What was it like for Andrew (and the others) to be left out of those moments? Were there flickers of envy? Were harsh words or suspicious innuendoes shared?

Those are all human reactions to very real situations. Fortunately the gospel calls us, as it called them, to transcend those earthly feelings. Perhaps that is why none of that is recorded for us. It wasn't worthy. The gospel makes it clear that it is Jesus who counts.

Peter and Andrew, as well as the other apostles, are noted by the evangelist because of their quick, unquestioning response to the summons of Jesus to follow him. That's all that mattered. First-born rights, age, superior business acumen, none of that matters with Jesus. All that counts is hearing his word, his call to holiness, and then responding wholeheartedly. The blustery fishermen-brothers of Galilee are commended for that.

In our own time, fame, prosperity, titles, and accomplishments do not matter either. Andrew may have been related to Peter. If the two brothers supported each other in life and in faith, that is a noble and memorable reality. But something matters more than that: Jesus. It was faith in Jesus that made them important. We share that same faith. In God's vision, we are important because of our response to Jesus. That is what matters.

Prayer
Lord God, it is so easy for envy to creep into our lives. We look at others whose lives seem easier, wealthier, happier. We wonder why that good fortune isn't our own. This feast of Saint Andrew calls me to be better than all that, to recognize that one thing counts: your son, Jesus. Andrew was his follower. So am I. Help me to follow more closely, to listen more carefully to the gospel, to deepen my faith in Jesus. Amen.

Saint Nicholas
December 6

Isaiah 6:1–8 • John 10:11–16

The current abbot of the Dormition Abbey in Jerusalem is named Nicholas. It is an appropriate name for this kindly Benedictine monk who has a great love of the eastern ecclesiastical traditions.

The feast day of Nicholas is well celebrated in this monastery. The evening meal, a rather simple affair most other days, is replete with wine and many courses. After the meal there is a party. The university students at the monastery present skits and songs, many of them, in fine student tradition, poking fun at the foibles of the monks. Old Brother Hilarion dresses as Saint Nicholas, wearing the abbot's miter and carrying his crosier. His own lengthy beard is testament to his wisdom; his twinkling eyes, a witness to his kindness.

There is something very special about this evening, as there is about this venerable saint. It is appropriate that the feast of Saint Nicholas should occur during Advent. In many parts of the world where commercialism hasn't yet dented the holiness of the season, this is the day on which gifts are exchanged. With all the gift-giving out of the way, the believer is able to put a different kind of spotlight on Christmas, to celebrate the Incarnation of Jesus, and not the revelry of secular society.

Nicholas himself has been a victim of history. There are more legends than facts recorded about the man. We know he was a bishop in Myra (Turkey). We know that he attended the important ecumenical council of Nicea, and that he died about the year 350.

Legends tells of his kindness: He provided dowries for poor girls, hence he is often depicted with a bag of gold in his hand. He is also the patron of sailors.

His name has been altered by various national groups. The Dutch Sinter Klaas has become our Santa Claus, a totally secular fellow whose only common trait with the true Nicholas is as a generous giver and lover of children.

Sometimes it is a pity that reality gets obscured with the passage of time. The secular Santa Claus is a far cry from the wise and generous bishop of Myra, whose whole life was dedicated to God's great gift of Jesus. Nonetheless, this feast falls early in our Advent season. Perhaps we can be wise enough to use this day to clarify for ourselves the need to give the true meaning of Christmas.

Surprise someone today with a gift or phone call in honor of Saint Nicholas.

Prayer

Lord God, how history has changed this saint! How used he is by our commercial world! Help me in the rush of this season to keep the perspective that Nicholas had, to give simple gifts and not to forget the poor who get no gifts. Open my heart to generous love and let my eyes twinkle with kindness for others, especially those who try my patience. Keep me mindful that the real gift of this season is your gift of Jesus. Amen.

Immaculate Conception
December 8

Genesis 3:9–15, 20 • Ephesians 1:3–6, 11–12
Luke 1:26–38

One of the characteristics of our modern technological way of life is the reality that we can switch gears easily. A tape player can reverse direction with the push of a button. Our cars can reverse direction considerably more easily than can a horse and buggy.

The ability to change is especially important when we realize that sometimes we are headed in the wrong direction. We need to turn around. Sometimes quite quickly. We need to go the right way.

That is one of the lessons we can learn from this Solemnity of the Immaculate Conception. The first reading tells us the familiar story of Genesis, of a man and a woman who were headed in the wrong direction. Like us, they were not evil. Like us, they made choices. Here, they made a bad one, a decision that sent all humanity careening on a course of disaster. As a result of their one incorrect decision, more choices for selfishness, indulgence, and sin resulted. The story in Genesis tells us that it was the fault of Eve, but behind the story is the sad reality that it is telling a tale of all humanity, of you and of me, and of the selfish, hurting decisions that we make.

It might seem like nothing could reverse this. Prophets and wise teachers could not convince the people to turn around, to go another way. The bible tells the story of the few people who learned in time, and the many people who never learned, whose decisions cost lives, nations, and worst of all, souls.

Today, on this Solemnity of the Immaculate Conception, we read about another woman. Like Eve, like us, she had to make decisions. Like us, the times in which she lived were not so good, nor so bad. But unlike Eve and unlike us, when God chose to act with power and with mystery in her life, she responded simply and faithfully: "Let it be done to me as you say." That simple sentence, that declaration of trust in God—even though she did not understand all that it meant or all that it would do to her—was all that was necessary to reverse the disastrous path humanity had chosen in Genesis. In fact, to symbolize the reversal of direction, medieval theologians took the name "Eva" (Eve) and spelled it backwards, forming the word "Ave" (in English: "hail") the first word of the prayer we associate with Mary, the Hail Mary.

We celebrate this feast because it demonstrates human possibility at its finest. It is not because Mary's example is aloof from human experience, but because Mary's sinless conception and life reversed Eve's sin. We, too, can reverse the patterns of our lives that lead us away from God, away from Paradise, away from God's kingdom, and away from one another.

Our own stories will probably not be recorded like those of Eve or Mary. But our personal story will be remembered by God. With Mary, the maiden of Nazareth, we ask for the grace to be honest with ourselves and with God, to let God's power into our lives, to say "Let it be done to me as you say," and to mean it!

Prayer

Lord God, you chose Mary to be the mother of your Son. You let her live in our world and know our human condition, yet she was able to transcend all the pettiness and selfishness and sin that mar our lives. On this Solemnity of the Immaculate Conception help me to imitate this woman of faith. Let me say, "Let it be done to me as you say." Let me say "yes" to your love and to your will for my life. Amen.

Our Lady of Guadalupe
December 12

Zechariah 2:14–17 • Revelation 11:19;12:1–6,10 •
Luke 1:39–47

Advent is a season for Mary. From beginning to end the events that touched her life are brought to mind in readings, in art, in Christmas cards, and in the songs of the season. It is appropriate that this feast occur in the season of Advent.

Europe is the location of the great appearances associated with Mary in this century. So much of Western religious history did not originate in the Americas, but was brought to this side of the ocean by the early explorers and settlers. The strong influence of that faith is seen throughout the Americas. The story of Our Lady of Guadalupe is an exception. It is perhaps the most famous example of Mary's presence in North America.

The story goes like this: An Indian boy who lived near Mexico City was on his way to Mass one morning when he heard a voice calling his name. Juan Diego climbed the knoll and saw a beautiful woman who ordered that he intercede with the local bishop to build a church at this high place.

Juan Diego obeyed the order and went to the bishop, but the bishop did not believe him. He asked for a sign.

Don't we all always ask for a sign? Somehow faith is not enough. It seems easier if there is tangible evidence.

On his way to church again, the lad passed the same hill where the same beautiful woman appeared to him. The sign she offered was simple. She told the lad to pluck some of the local flowers and take them to the bishop in his cloak. Again, he did as he was told.

When he arrived at the bishop's residence he opened his

cloak to present the simple gift of the flowers, but instead of the flowers there was an image of the Mother of God on his cloak. It is this image which is honored as Our Lady of Guadalupe.

The church was built as Mary had requested. It continues to draw pilgrims by the thousands each day. All this occurred shortly after the Spanish invasion of Mexico. The sign was given not to one of the learned missionaries, but to a humble peasant of the land. His action and the story surrounding it have been a foundation stone of faith for the people of Mexico and those of Hispanic descent throughout the Americas.

It seems that God always chooses such unlikely candidates to be the agents of revelation. As we make our way through Advent we might be tempted to look for signs, too. Instead, we should look at the people around us. Like Juan Diego, they are God's sign.

Prayer

Lord God, it would all be so much easier if you would just give me a sign of what to do or what to choose. But then it wouldn't be faith any more, would it? It would be proof. Help me to see the signs that you have already given to me, the signs of your love active in other people—and in myself. Let your sacraments and your word be your greatest sign to me. Amen.

Saint Lucy
December 13

Song of Songs 8:6–7 • Matthew 25:1–13

Many years ago I had the chance to visit Venice. Its quiet canals and waterways certainly helped me to understand its traditional name of "Most Serene Republic." The absence of motor vehicle traffic and noise was a welcome relief from the usually crowded conditions of other major European cities.

In the evening my friends and I went to a small pub. We each ordered a beer and some pretzels. Later, when the bill came, we were charged over $50 (U.S.) for this light snack. I mustered my finest Italian to ask why it was so expensive and to express my outrage, but the owner simply shrugged and said, "You ask the band to play *Santa Lucia.*" It was a dear price to experience the traditional song of the Venetian gondoliers.

Lucia, or Lucy, has been a favorite saint of Christians from the earliest days of the church. In an age when virginity was highly prized among members of the Christian community Lucy gave up her life rather than marry. It would be tempting to say much more about the topic of sexuality and virginity in this day and age, but that would miss the point of her inclusion in Advent.

Lucy means light. Centuries ago, before the reform of the calendar by Pope Gregory, her feast fell on the longest night of winter. Light and darkness. That is so much a part of Advent, isn't it? The very name "Lucy" helped to melt away some of that winter darkness. The memory of Lucy helps to thaw some of the ice-cold nature of sin that marks our lives and that blocks Jesus from coming to us fully.

In northern Europe great fires are lit on this feast of light. These immense bonfires illuminate the winter night and bring warmth to cold bodies and souls. Jesus, the light, is coming into the world. The feast of Lucy is a forerunner to the great feast of Christmas.

Advent is filled with both heroes and heroines, men and women of courage and faith: Isaiah, John the Baptizer, Elizabeth, and Mary. Today we pause to remember another young woman of faith. In the darkest moments of our own lives, we can turn to Lucy and ask for a measure of her courage and faith, and a ray of her light.

Prayer

Lord God, you chose Lucy to give witness to you and to be an example for the church. You choose us, too. Just as her feast helps to light the darkness of winter, may our example add to the brightness of the Advent candles in our homes. Let my example of faith be a light to others. Let my love bring warmth to faith's winter. Amen.

Of Related Interest...

Scripture Reflections Day by Day
Rev. Joseph Donders

These gospel meditations are current, timely, short enough to be read in any free moment and full of meaning and hope.

ISBN: 0-89622-494-5, 384 pp, $9.95

Refreshment in the Desert
Gilbert Padilla

Forty-two short, easy-to-read meditations that explore the gospel messages of charity, love, forgiveness and prayer.

ISBN: 0-89622-228-4, 128 pp, $7.95

The Coming of the Lord
A Guide to the Sunday Readings for Advent and the Christmas Season
J.D. Crichton

The book offers commentary on the origins of Advent, Christmas, and Epiphany and the lectionary texts for all three cycles.

ISBN: 0-89622-461-9, 96 pp, $5.95

Available at religious bookstores or from

TWENTY-THIRD PUBLICATIONS
P.O. Box 180 • Mystic, CT 06355
1-800-321-0411